Team Building

Second Edition

Team Building

Issues and Alternatives

William G. Dyer
Brigham Young University

 Addison-Wesley Publishing Company
Reading, Massachusetts • Menlo Park, California • Don Mills, Ontario
• Wokingham, England • Amsterdam • Sydney • Singapore • Tokyo
• Madrid • Bogotá • Santiago • San Juan

This book is in the Addison-Wesley Series on Organization
Development.
Editors: Edgar H. Schein, Richard Beckhard

Other titles in the series:

Organizational Transitions:
Managing Complex Change, Second Edition
Richard Beckhard and Reuben Harris

Organization Development:
A Normative View
W. Warner Burke

The Technology Connection:
Strategy and Change in the Information Age
Marc S. Gerstein

Stream Analysis:
A Powerful Way to Diagnose and Manage Organizational Change
Jerry I. Porras

Process Consultation Volume II:
Lessons for Managers and Consultants
Edgar H. Schein

Managing Conflict:
Interpersonal Dialogue and Third-Party Roles,
Second Edition
Richard E. Walton

Library of Congress Cataloging-in-Publication Data

Dyer, William G.
  Team building.

  (The Addison-Wesley series on organization development)
  Includes bibliographical references.
  1. Work groups. 2. Organizational change.
I. Title. II. Series.
HD66.D94 1987   658.4′02   86–20635
ISBN 0–201–18037–5

Reprinted with corrections June, 1987

CDEFGHIJ–BA–898

Foreword

The Addison-Wesley Series on Organization Development originated in the late 1960s when a number of us recognized that the rapidly growing field of "OD" was not well understood or well defined. We also recognized that there was no one OD philosophy, and hence one could not at that time write a textbook on the theory and practice of OD, but one could make clear what various practitioners were doing under that label. So the original six books by Beckhard, Bennis, Blake and Mouton, Lawrence and Lorsch, Schein, and Walton launched what has since become a continuing enterprise. The essence of this enterprise was to let different authors speak for themselves instead of trying to summarize under one umbrella what was obviously a rapidly growing and highly diverse field.

By 1981 the series included nineteen titles, having added books by Beckhard and Harris, Cohen and Gadon, Davis, Dyer, Galbraith, Hackman and Oldham, Heenan and Perlmutter, Kotter, Lawler, Nadler, Roeber, Schein, and Steele. This proliferation reflected what had happened to the field of OD. It was growing by leaps and bounds, and it was expanding into all kinds of organizational areas and technologies of intervention. By this time many textbooks existed as well that tried to capture the core concepts of the field, but we felt that diversity and innovation were still the more salient aspects of OD today.

The present series is an attempt both to recapture some basics and to honor the growing diversity. So we have begun a series of revisions of some of the original books and have added a set of new authors or old authors with new content. Our hope is to capture the spirit of inquiry and innovation that has always been the hallmark of organizational development and to launch with these books a new wave of insights into the forever tricky problem of how to change and improve organizations.

We are grateful that Addison-Wesley has chosen to continue the series and are also grateful to the many reviewers who have helped us and the authors in the preparation of the current series of books.

Cambridge, Massachusetts   Edgar H. Schein
New York, New York   Richard Beckhard

Preface

After being deeply involved for nearly twenty-five years in conducting team-building sessions for organizations, there are still some conditions that are a puzzle to me. In a recent management conference with which I worked, I asked 300 managers from a variety of organizations how many of them felt that teamwork, people cooperating to achieve goals, was essential in their organization and their own work unit. Every manager indicated that teamwork was essential. Then I asked, "How many of you have ever conducted some type of program to ensure that your team was functioning effectively?" Fewer than 25% indicated that they had ever done any regular program of team building. Next I asked, "You belong to another team managed by your boss. How many of your bosses have ever conducted a program to help develop this work unit?" Between 10% and 15% indicated that their bosses had taken some action in this area.

The puzzle to me, and the reason I am revising my book on team building, is that almost every manager in almost every organization supports teamwork. In fact, many feel it is essential. But very few organizations institute an organizationwide program to ensure team effectiveness, and relatively few managers start the process on their own without organizational support. This increases my feeling that managers at all levels must learn how to overcome the resistance to instituting a systematic team-building process, and must know how to go about conducting such a program.

Almost every current book on effective organizations has emphasized the crucial importance of teamwork.[1] My own recent research of 200 companies across the United States confirms that organizations do realize that well-functioning teams can produce results. Yet few organizations carry out a systematic program for developing organization teams. It is as though they feel that people ought to know how to work together without any formal training or development activity. And it is true that some managers have a personal "feel" for how to work with people to produce team effort. But many more do not. They do not know how to start up a new team in a way that will maximize the possibility of good teamwork, how to check to see if any problems are developing, and how to deal with team problems when they occur.

This book is written for managers who want to know how to get a more systematic program of team building moving in their organization or unit. It is also designed to help professional consultants or human resource specialists who assist managers in team-building programs to understand the dynamics of doing effective team building.

As I have talked with managers and workers over the past years, I have been impressed that people do seem to be aware of the unsatisfying nature of work activity when they do not feel there is any "teamwork" or "team spirit." They may not be able to define clearly what a good team includes, but they have a sense or a feeling about a unit that is not working as a team. What do people say about poor teamwork? They say things like

> It's no fun working with those people. They just seem to be so involved in their own work that they don't want to do anything for anyone else.

> Our meetings are chaos. When we get together and try to get work accomplished, nobody listens—we fight and argue and nobody supports anyone else.

> We never do anything that is teamlike. We don't set goals,

---

[1] See T. Peter and R. Waterman, *In Search of Excellence* (New York: Harper & Row, 1982), esp. pp. 126–127; W. Ouchi, *Theory Z* (New York: Avon, 1981), p. 66; D. Clifford and R. Cavanagh, *The Winning Performance* (New York: Bantam, 1985), p. 135; and M. Moskowitz, "Lessons from the Best Companies to Work For," *California Management Review* (Winter 1985): 42–47.

we don't plan, we don't do work together. Everything is done in one-on-one meetings with the boss. When we have staff meetings it is just one person at a time talking to the boss while the rest listen.

I don't trust anyone in that bunch I work with. They would all knife you in the back if they thought it would help their cause. At times they can act so friendly, but when the crunch comes it is each person for himself.

People talk about teamwork around here but I don't know what that means. I go to work, I sit at my desk, and take care of my assignments. From time to time I go to meetings, which are usually a waste of time. I get a yearly performance review, which hasn't changed much in years, and I draw my pay. I don't see what teamwork means in my job.

There are some people I work with whom I really like and enjoy working with, but there are others who bother me and we don't get along. I find it easier to avoid them or get things done with as little interaction as possible.

My boss is so busy that he doesn't even talk about how our staff could become a team. He has his favorites whom he talks to, but the rest of us just do our work and hardly ever have any significant involvement with the boss.

Most people have had at least one work experience they felt was "a real good team," and they compare the existing situation with that point of reference in the past. Some people claim they have *never* been a part of a satisfying work team and do not think they could describe an effective team. It is difficult for people in the latter category to engage in and sustain a team-building program since they really do not know what they are trying to achieve. The first group feels they know what real teamwork "feels" like, but they are often not sure what kind of actions are needed to reproduce what they had once experienced.

The most critical factor in starting a team-building program is the degree of commitment of the unit managers and members to building a better work team. I have become wary of working with a group on team building if the leader is suspicious, unconvinced, halfhearted, or engaging in the activity because of pressure from above. I want to hear the manager, as he or she talks to the subordinates, say something like,

> I want this work group to be as good as it can be. There are some things that go on that keep us from being as effective as we could be. That disturbs me, and it disturbs me that I may be part of the problem. But I am willing to spend my time, energy, and resources to make this group as effective as possible, and I am willing to make needed changes. I need to know how you feel about engaging in a team-building activity. What are your real feelings? I don't think we ought to start unless all of us are truly committed to the activity.

It is possible, even with this approach and the commitment of leaders and members, that the team-building program will fail. Sometimes key people leave; sometimes the problems are too deep or complex. It is possible that the approach may not be right or the facilitator does not have enough skill. But without commitment to engage in the process, deeply and honestly, everything could be in order and still nothing would change. So I seek commitment in my team-building work. I feel commitment increases if people know what is going to happen and if the process makes sense. But after reviewing the approach and providing all the insight I can, then I want to know about people's commitment. For me, testing commitment is an art, not a science. I cannot measure whether a person is a 6 or an 8 on a commitment scale, because I do not have a scale. I have to talk and listen to others talk and trust my experience and judgment. I judge commitment, to some degree, by the willingness of the leader and unit members to take responsibility for team-building work, to spend time, to accept assignments, and to get involved in the agreed-on actions. Team building is a human process. It involves human feelings, attitudes, and actions. It is something that people have to accomplish among themselves. You cannot substitute high-paid consultants, complex designs, or fancy resorts for human beings making a mutual commitment to try to work together more effectively.

Provo, Utah   W. G. D.

Contents

Team Building

Part I
What Team Development Is About

1

Teams Are Everywhere

Jim Thomas is manager of the Mountainside plant of the National Alloys Company. He has a tough production schedule that demands solid performance from all of his people, in all areas of the plant. Jim wants to do a top-flight job and becomes concerned when production drops, when problems go unsolved, or when morale sags.

After his job and his family, Jim's greatest interest is pro football — particularly as played by the Dallas Cowboys. Being a native Texan, Jim has followed the Dallas team from its inception. He gets to attend an occasional game and watches them regularly on television or listens to them on the radio. When the game is over, Jim can give a clear, detailed accounting for the team's success or failure.

What raises Jim's blood pressure to the boiling point is to watch the Cowboys fail to play as a team. He can spot in an instant when someone misses a block, loafs on the job, fails to pass on obvious information to the quarterback, or tries to shine at the expense of the team. He can diagnose the Cowboys' areas of weakness, and, if the coach could only hear him, he would tell him what to do to remedy the situation. But with all of his insight about teamwork and football, Jim fails to see the parallels between what is needed to improve the Dallas Cowboys and what is needed to shape up the management team at National Alloys. Many of the problems are exactly the same.

- Some individuals have never really learned what their assignments are, particularly for certain plays or situations.
- Some are afraid of the coach, so they pretend to know things that they should be asking questions about.
- Some want to do things "the old way," while others feel that more modern methods are needed.
- Factions and cliques quarrel and fight.
- The whole unit has not come together to develop common goals to which everyone is committed.
- Decisions are made by someone, but some people either don't "get the word" or they disagree silently with the decision and drag their feet.
- There is jealousy between units and a lack of playing together.
- Even when people are aware of a problem, they don't know exactly what to do about it.

Teams are collections of people who must rely on group collaboration if each member is to experience the optimum of success and goal achievement. It is obvious that in order to score touchdowns and prevent the opponent from scoring, a football team has to play together. It should be just as obvious that a work unit or a management group must also work together to ensure success. A football team practices over and over again how it will execute its plays. The team has "skull" practice, when they talk over plans and strategies. They review films of past games, identify mistakes, set up goals for the next week. Unfortunately, Jim Thomas's management group does not engage in any similar activities. They do not review their past actions and they do not really plan new strategies. They do not come together to learn from their mistakes, nor do they practice or get coaching on new methods, set new goals, or build team spirit. Jim Thomas can spot the absence of teamwork on the playing field but cannot see similar symptoms in the work plant. He is aware that sometimes things are not running smoothly at work, but he is unsure just what is wrong and he does not know what to do about it.

The Family Team

When Jim Thomas goes home at night, he enters into another "team," a most personal, sensitive, and important unit — his family. Here again is a group of people who must collaborate and combine resources in order that each group member may achieve his or her goals. Jim can easily sense when the right family spirit is missing. When his wife is upset or angry, when one of their children is troubled, or when Jim is tense and anxious, the entire family is affected. Morale droops. Here again, Jim is very sensitive to the interpersonal climate, but as in the work setting, he often feels helpless and inept when it comes to doing something about a problem situation.

Other Teams

If Jim would look more closely, he would be able to spot examples of human "teams" functioning either poorly or effectively all around him. At church, for example, Jim belongs to another team, the Planning and Finance Committee. He often is aware of long hours wasted in committee meetings because people are not prepared with reports that are needed, signals are not clear about assignments, decisions get "lost" and have to be made over again, or discussions bog down in fruitless arguments.

The community symphony orchestra chaired by Jim's wife is another team; like the Dallas Cowboys, they must practice to ensure a coordinated performance. Even Jim, who is no great connoisseur of music, is aware when the orchestra is not playing together. At the last concert there was an embarrassing silence when the drums failed to sound at a critical moment.

Jim likes to go to his favorite gas station because everyone pitches in to give customers quick, efficient service. One attendant takes care of the gas and checks under the hood, while the other cleans the windows and headlights. If anything needs changing, they bring it to Jim's attention, without high-pressuring for a sale. The employees help each other without being asked. "A good team," Jim thinks.

Many people are like Jim, only vaguely aware that modern society is a complex of interdependent groups or teams. People are called on to work with each other in a variety of situations, at work, home, schools, clubs, church, and community and service organizations. Just like a football or basketball team, these organizational teams can malfunction and fail to score or win, and for many of the same reasons. All teams need good coaching or management. There needs to be a review of past effort and rehearsal or replanning. Problems between members must be resolved; things that are unclear should be understood. Good teams stop and take stock of their performance, diagnose the problems, and then take actions to ensure that they will be ready to play the next game.

This book is about organizational teams, especially about what can be done to help a team diagnose its problems and act to develop into a more effective working unit. Managers are like coaches. They must be able to look at the team effort with a practiced eye, see what is interfering with maximum effort or find out what the blocks are, and then devise a strategy or plan to remove the obstacles and release people for maximum effort as they combine their resources to achieve common goals. That is the name of the game in team development.

Most managers are stopped from solving work unit problems either because they don't see what the real problems are or because they don't know exactly what to do. This book is intended to help managers overcome both these obstacles, by providing a sound basis for making a correct diagnosis and by outlining team-building procedures that have proven to be effective.

2

Emergence of the Team Idea

A breakthrough in organization theory and practice came in the late 1920s and early 1930s with the now classic Hawthorne Studies. This research, conducted by a group of Harvard University professors at the Hawthorne, Illinois plant of the Western Electric Company, started out to test the hypothesis that work output is connected with work-area lighting or illumination. It was hypothesized that workers would work more efficiently under conditions of good lighting, a hypothesis that stemmed from the stimulus–response theory that individuals respond directly to external stimuli; thus by controlling the stimuli, management hoped to control the workers' effort.

The first phase of research resulted in some puzzling data. The production output of the experimental subjects (the group working under altered lighting) constantly increased, even though lighting decreased. This led to a series of research activities designed to examine in depth what happens to a group of workers under various conditions. Six operators were selected to work in a special test group assembling telephone relays. Data were collected on this group for five years under a variety of conditions; rest periods and methods of pay were varied, refreshments and a shortened work week were tried, and so on. The researchers found

that work output seemed ultimately to be a function of something more than rest periods, incentives, or refreshments. After
much analysis, the researchers generally agreed that the most significant factor was the building of a sense of group identity, a
feeling of social support and cohesion that came with increased
worker interaction. Also, the superior or management leader was
observed to behave somewhat differently toward the workers in
the experimental group, and this, too, appeared to enhance the
team spirit.

Elton Mayo, one of the original researchers, summarized
the Hawthorne experiment this way:

> The original provisions were effective largely because the
> experimental room was in charge of *an interested and
> sympathetic chief observer.* He understood clearly from the
> first that any hint of "the supervisor" in his methods might
> be fatal to the interests of the inquiry. So far as it was pos-
> sible, he and his assistants kept the history sheets and the
> log sheet faithfully posted. In addition to this he *took a
> personal interest in each girl* and her achievement; *he
> showed pride in the record of the group.* He helped the
> group to feel that its duty was to *set its own conditions of
> work,* he helped the workers to find the "freedom" of which
> they so frequently speak.
>
> In the early stages of development, it was inevitable that
> the group should become interested in its achievement and
> should to some extent enjoy the reflected glory of the in-
> terest the inquiry attracted. As the years passed this abated
> somewhat, but all the evidence — including the mainte-
> nance of a high output — goes to show that something in
> the reconditioning of the group must be regarded as a per-
> manent achievement. At no time in the five-year period did
> the girls feel that they were working under pressure; on the
> contrary, they invariably cite the absence of this as their
> reason for preferring the "test room."
>
> Undoubtedly, there had been a remarkable change of
> mental attitude in the group. This showed in their recur-
> rent conferences with high executive authorities. At first
> shy and uneasy, silent and perhaps somewhat suspicious of

the company's intention, later their attitude is marked by confidence and candor. *Before every change of program, the group is consulted.* Their comments are listened to and discussed; sometimes their objectives are allowed to negate a suggestion. *The group unquestionably develops a sense of participation in the critical determinations and becomes something of a social unit.*[1](Emphasis added.)

The Hawthorne study illustrates some of the elements essential for team effectiveness, because the experiment showed the possibility of taking a random collection of employees and building them into a highly productive work team. Mayo's discussion points out certain critical factors:

1. The boss (chief observer) had a personal interest in each person's achievement.
2. He took pride in the record of the group.
3. He helped the group work together to set its own conditions of work.
4. He faithfully posted the feedback on performance.
5. The group took pride in its own achievement and had the satisfaction of outsiders showing interest in what they did.
6. The group did not feel they were being pressured to change.
7. Before changes were made, the group was consulted.
8. The group developed a sense of confidence and candor.

These conditions for developing an effective work team, identified in a research effort begun in 1928, are still important considerations for managers nearly sixty years later.

Group Concepts in Management

Two of the early writers in the area of management who began to emphasize the team concept as an important part of

---

[1]Elton Mayo, *The Human Problems of an Industrial Civilization* (Boston: Division of Research, Graduate School of Business Administration, Harvard University, 1933). Quoted with permission.

management theory were Douglas McGregor and Rensis Likert. In the last chapter of *The Human Side of Enterprise*, McGregor discussed the managerial team. He describes a highly effective management team studied by researchers and notes the researchers' conclusion that "unity of purpose" was the main distinguishing characteristic of this successful unit.

> The significance of unity of purpose within a managerial team is given some lip service by most managers, but it is not always recognized that this objective can only be achieved by a closely knit *group*. Most so-called managerial teams are not teams at all, but collections of individual relationships with the boss in which each individual is vying with each other for power, prestige, recognition, and personal autonomy. Under such conditions unity of purpose is a myth.
>
> One research study of top management groups found that 85 percent of the communications within the groups took place between individual subordinates and the superior (up *and* down), and only 15 percent laterally between the subordinates. Many executives who talk about their "teams" of subordinates would be appalled to discover how low is the actual level of collaboration among them, and how high is the mutual suspicion and antagonism. Yet these same executives generally create the very conditions which would appall them if recognized. They do so by managing individuals rather than helping to create a genuine group.[2]

At the time McGregor was writing, William W. Whyte had just written a book, *Organizational Man*, in which he decried the use of groups in organizations, claiming the group activities had a depressing or leveling effect on individual performance and stultified creativity and individual expression. McGregor commented:

> These views [of Whyte] deny the realities of organizational life. Many activities simply cannot be carried on and many

[2]Douglas McGregor, *The Human Side of Enterprise* (New York: McGraw-Hill, 1960), pp. 228–229. Copyright © 1960 by McGraw-Hill Book Company. Used with permission of McGraw-Hill Book Company.

problems cannot be solved on an individual basis or in two person relationships. . . .

In general we are remarkably inept in accomplishing objectives through group effort. This is not inevitable. It is a result of inadequate understanding and skill with respect to the unique aspects of group operation.

Whyte's thesis that we have given undue emphasis to group phenomena, and in the process lost track of individuals, misses the point altogether. The real problem is that we have given so little attention to group behavior that management does not know enough about how to create the conditions for individual growth and integrity in the group situation. The problem is one of ignorance based on under, not overemphasis.[3]

McGregor then identified the characteristics of an effective work team (see Figure 2–1).

At the same time McGregor's book was having its impact, Likert, in *New Patterns of Management,* was developing his notion of organizations as a series of interlocking groups and the manager as a "linking pin." As he studied the research literature, Likert felt that managers must learn to cope with a totality of people under their direction and not just manage individuals one-to-one. Likert's ideal form of management (System 4) is called "Participative Group" management.[4] Likert identified twenty-four properties and performance characteristics of the ideal, highly effective group, as noted in Figure 2–2.

Blake and Mouton have widely used the team analogy in describing their "9,9 management":

Because the work team is likely to be used to refer to any set of individuals who cooperate in accomplishing a single overall result, the question can be asked whether team action of the kind being described leads to conformity pressures which dampen individuality and stifle independence of effort. The answer is that the opposite is true. True team

---

[3]Ibid., pp. 229–230.
[4]Rensis Likert, *New Patterns of Management* (New York: McGraw-Hill, 1961).

Figure 2–1

McGregor's Characteristics of an Effective Work Team

1. The "atmosphere" tends to be informal, comfortable, relaxed. There are no obvious tensions. It is a working atmosphere in which people are involved and interested. There are no signs of boredom.

2. There is a lot of discussion in which virtually everyone participates, but it remains pertinent to the task of the group. If the discussion gets off the subject, someone will bring it back in short order.

3. The task or the objective of the group is well understood and accepted by the members. There will have been free discussion of the objective at some point, until it was formulated in such a way that the members of the group could commit themselves to it.

4. The members listen to each other! The discussion does not have the quality of jumping from one idea to another unrelated one. Every idea is given a hearing. People do not appear to be afraid of being foolish by putting forth a creative thought even if it seems fairly extreme.

5. There is disagreement. The group is comfortable with this and shows no signs of having to avoid conflict or to keep everything on the plane of sweetness and light. Disagreements are not suppressed or overridden by premature group action. The reasons are carefully examined, and the group seeks to resolve them rather than to dominate the dissenter.

   On the other hand, there is no "tyranny of the minority." Individuals who disagree do not appear to be trying to dominate the group or to express hostility. Their disagreement is an expression of a genuine difference of opinion, and they expect a hearing in order that a solution may be found.

   Sometimes there are basic disagreements which cannot be resolved. The group finds it possible to live with them, accepting them but not permitting them to block its efforts. Under some conditions, action will be deferred to permit further study of an issue between the members. On other occasions, where the disagreement cannot be resolved and action is necessary, it will be taken but with open caution and recognition that the action may be subject to later reconsideration.

6. Most decisions are reached by a kind of consensus in which it is clear that everybody is in general agreement and willing to go along. However, there is little tendency for individuals who oppose the action to keep their opposition private and thus let an apparent consensus

Figure 2-1 *(cont.)*

mask real disagreement. Formal voting is at a minimum; the group does not accept a simple majority as a proper basis for action.

7. Criticism is frequent, frank, and relatively comfortable. There is little evidence of personal attack, either openly or in a hidden fashion. The criticism has a constructive flavor in that it is oriented toward removing an obstacle that faces the group and prevents it from getting the job done.

8. People are free in expressing their feelings as well as their ideas both on the problem and on the group's operation. There is little pussyfooting, there are few "hidden agendas." Everybody appears to know quite well how everybody else feels about any matter under discussion.

9. When action is taken, clear assignments are made and accepted.

10. The chairman of the group does not dominate it, nor on the contrary, does the group defer unduly to him or her. In fact, as one observes the activity, it is clear that the leadership shifts from time to time, depending on the circumstances. Different members, because of their knowledge or experience, are in a position at various times to act as "resources" for the group. The members utilize them in this fashion and they occupy leadership roles while they are thus being used. There is little evidence of a struggle for power as the group operates. The issue is not who controls, but how to get the job done.

11. The group is self-conscious about its own operations. Frequently, it will stop to examine how well it is doing or what may be interfering with its operation. The problem may be a matter or procedure, or it may be an individual whose behavior is interfering with the accomplishment of the group's objectives. Whatever it is, it gets open discussion until a solution is found.

action is more like a football situation where division of effort is meshed into a single coordinated result; where the whole is more, and different, than the sum of its individual parts. Here, there is a common set of signals, based on understanding, which dictate action — a division of closely knitted individual activity combined with interdependent

Figure 2–2
Likert's Characteristics of an Effective Work Group

---

1. Members are skilled in all the various leadership and membership roles and functions required for interaction between leaders and members and between members and other members.

2. The group has been in existence sufficiently long to have developed a well-established, relaxed working relationship among all its members.

3. The members of the group are attracted to it and are loyal to its members, including the leader.

4. The members and leaders have a high degree of confidence and trust in each other.

5. The values and goals of the group are a satisfactory integration and expression of the relevant values and needs of its members. They have helped shape these values and goals and are satisfied with them.

6. Insofar as members of the group are performing linking functions, they endeavor to have the values and goals of the groups which they link in harmony, one with the other.

7. The more important a value seems to the group, the greater the likelihood that the individual members will accept it.

8. The members of the group are highly motivated to abide by the major values and to achieve the important goals of the group. Each member will do all that he or she reasonably can — and at times all in his or her power — to help the group achieve its central objectives. Each member expects every other member to do the same.

9. All the interaction, problem-solving, decision-making activities of the group occur in a supportive atmosphere. Suggestions, comments, ideas, information, criticisms are all offered with a helpful orientation. Similarly, these contributions are received in the same spirit. Respect is shown for the point of view of others, both in the way contributions are made and in the way they are received.

10. The superior of each work group exerts a major influence in establishing the tone and atmosphere of that work group by his or her leadership principles and practices. In the highly effective group, consequently, the leader adheres to those principles of leadership which create a supportive atmosphere in the group and a cooperative rather than a competitive relationship among the members.

11. The group is eager to help each member develop to his or her full potential. It sees, for example, that relevant technical knowledge and

---

Figure 2-2 *(cont.)*

training in interpersonal and group skills are made available to each member.

12. Each member accepts willingly and without resentment the goals and expectations that the individual and the group establish for themselves. The anxieties, fears, and emotional stresses produced by direct pressure for high performance from a boss in a hierarchical situation are not present. Groups seem capable of setting high performance goals for the group as a whole and for each member. These goals are high enough to stimulate each member to do his or her best, but not so high as to create anxieties or fear of failure. In an effective group, each person can exert sufficient influence on the decisions of the group to prevent the group from setting unattainable goals for any member while setting high goals for all. The goals are adapted to the member's capacity to perform.

13. The leader and the members believe that each group member can accomplish the "impossible." The expectations stretch each member to the maximum and accelerate personal growth. When necessary, the group tempers the expectation level so that the member is not broken by a feeling of failure or rejection.

14. When necessary or advisable, other members of the group will give a member the help needed to accomplish successfully the goals set for that person. Mutual help is a characteristic of highly effective groups.

15. The supportive atmosphere of the highly effective group stimulates creativity. The group does not demand narrow conformity as do the work groups under authoritarian leaders. No one has to "yes the boss," nor is a person rewarded for such an attempt. The group attaches high value to new, creative approaches and solutions to its problems and to the problems of the organization of which it is a part.

16. The group knows the value of "constructive" conformity and knows when to use it and for what purposes. Although it does not permit conformity to affect adversely the creative efforts of its members, it does expect conformity on mechanical and administrative matters to save the time of members and to facilitate the group's activities.

17. There is strong motivation on the part of each member to communicate fully and frankly to the group all the information which is relevant and of value to the group's activity.

18. There is high motivation in the group to use the communication process so that it best serves the interests and goals of the group.

(cont.)

Figure 2–2 *(cont.)*

Every item which a member feels is important, but which for some reason is being ignored, will be repeated until it receives the attention that it deserves. Members strive also to avoid communicating unimportant information so as not to waste the group's time.

19. Just as there is high motivation to communicate, there is correspondingly strong motivation to receive communications. Each member is genuinely interested in any information on any relevant matter that any member of the group can provide. This information is welcomed and trusted as being honestly and sincerely given. Members do not look "behind" information and attempt to interpret it in ways opposite to its purported intent.

20. In the highly effective group, there are strong motivations to try to influence other members as well as to be receptive to influence by them. This applies to all the group's activities: technical matters, methods, organizational problems, interpersonal relationships, and group processes.

21. The group processes of the highly effective group enable the members to exert more influence on the leader and to communicate far more information to him or her, including suggestions as to what needs to be done and how the leader could do a better job, than is possible in a one-to-one relationship. By "tossing the ball" back and forth among the members, a group can communicate information to the leader which no single person on a one-to-one basis dare do.

22. The ability of the members of a group to influence each other contributes to the flexibility and adaptability of the group. Ideas, goals, and attitudes do not become frozen if members are able to influence each other continuously.

23. In the highly effective group, individual members feel secure in making decisions which seem appropriate to them because the goals and philosophy of operation are clearly understood by each member and provide a solid base for making decisions. This unleashes initiative and pushes decisions down while still maintaining a coordinated and direct effort.

24. The leader of a highly effective group is selected carefully. His or her leadership ability is so evident that he or she would probably emerge as a leader in any unstructured situation. To increase the likelihood that persons of high leadership competence are selected, the organization is likely to use peer nominations and related methods in selecting group leaders.

---

effort is the 9,9 pattern of integrating individual with organizational effort.[5]

They point out that a good team has task specialization and division of labor.

Each person shoulders a different part of the total job, with each having 100 percent responsibility for success of the whole. . . . Furthermore, it has in common a set of strategies to fit a variety of situations and signals which are well understood . . . and includes:

1. Team action based on synchronized effort of all.
2. Pair action, i.e., based on meshing of effort between coach-quarterback, quarterback-center, etc.
3. Solo effort, i.e., broken field running, pass interception, etc.[6]

How do you go about training managers to manage teams? Blake and Mouton state:

The question becomes, How do organizations which recognize the importance of team action go about training to get it?

A simple answer can be given by analogy to a baseball or football team. Both of these are organizations in a very real sense, and both are concerned with team action. Ridiculous though it sounds, if the conventional approach of training individuals one-by-one were applied in developing a baseball or a football team, each of the team members would be trained at the hands of specialists, also one-by-one, away from the organization and isolated from the others with whom he must eventually engage in team action. Then, all membeers would be returned to the organization and thrown together on the assumption that since all had learned individually, they automatically would be able to work together effectively. There would literally be no need for practice, and no one would think to help the team de-

[5]Robert Blake and Jane Mouton, *The Managerial Grid* (Houston: Gulf, 1964).

[6]Ibid., p. 153.

velop a set of common signals, because each person should have learned all that he needed to learn in his own specialized training program in order to become an effective member.

The absurdity of this can further be seen in the analogy of the football team where each designated individual would gain specialized training in schools, one school concerned with training guards, another with centers, etc. After persons had been trained individually, they would be returned to the football club for the purpose of playing together in the belief that an effective team operation would result after skills of individuals had been perfected. Both of these examples point to the fallacy in logic of a conventional approach to training when the goal of organizational health is successful team action.[7]

In a more recent analysis, still following the notion of the athletic team, Robert Keidal has identified the close parallel between the variation in sports teams and the variety in the organizational setting.[8] He uses baseball, football, and basketball teams to show some of the differences. Baseball, he says, is somewhat like a sales organization. Team members are relatively independent of one another and while all members are required to be on the field together, they virtually never interact together all at the same time.

Football is quite different. There are really three subteams within the total team — offense, defense, and the special team. When the subteam is on the field, every player is involved in every play, which is not the case in baseball. But the teamwork required is centered in the subteam, not the total team.

Basketball is an even different breed. Here the team is small, all players play on only one team. Every player is involved in all aspects of the game, offense and defense, and all must pass,

---

[7]R. R. Blake, J. S. Mouton, and M. G. Blansfield, "How Executive Team Training Can Help You." Reproduced by special permission from the January 1962 *Training and Development Journal* 16, 1, 1962. Copyright 1962 by the American Society for Training and Development, Inc.

[8]R. W. Keidal, "Baseball, Football, and Basketball: Models for Business," *Organizational Dynamics* (Winter 1984).

run, shoot. When a substitute comes in, all must play with the new person.

Keidal points out that organizational teams can vary just as athletic teams are different. This means the demands on the manager or leader will vary depending on the characteristics of the team and the general structure of the task, goals, and situation. For example, the major demands on the baseball coach are to develop short-term, game-by-game tactics. The manager's ability to develop an overall game plan (strategy) is limited. Management actions come in making quick key decisions about when to put in a relief pitcher or a pinch hitter.

On the other hand, the football coach must develop a game strategy as well as make some tactical decisions. The basketball coach will work with an entire team, since it is small, while the football coach must rely on a staff of assistants to handle various groups. The head football coach has the responsibility of building the staff of assistant coaches into its own team.

Since teams are different, the kind of team building needed varies. It is important to make a good diagnosis of the conditions that affect the team and the kinds of problems a team faces before launching into a team-building program. Besides the issues of teamness, and the structural demands, teams vary along a range of dimensions such as goals or immediate targets or pressures. Football teams face more pressure in each game, for example, than baseball teams; both are trying to win a championship, but a professional football team plays only about 15 games whereas a baseball team plays 100. Teams also differ as to size, longevity (some will last for years, while for others, such as task forces, the life span is only a few months), characteristics of members (in some teams all members are Ph.D.s, in others they are high school graduates), intensity of interactions and frequency of interaction, importance of the team to team members (one's family is obviously more important than membership in a volunteer group for neighborhood clean-up). It would appear that a high-intensity, high-interaction, long-term, very important team should be very concerned about making sure it is working together well and having the kind of impact needed on each team member. Team building would seem to be more critical for this team than for a team that meets infrequently and has limited goals of rather low salience for team members.

3

Team Building

How the Concept Has Matured

Team building grew out of the group dynamic's area of social psychology, incorporating much of the theory and research in small groups as well as the applied focus used in training groups (T-groups), which were very strong in the 1950s and 1960s. In the beginning the emphasis was on looking at the social interaction and relationships between people. This was consistent with management orientation at the time. During the late 1950s and early 1960s, management theory centered on the works of McGregor, Likert, and Blake and Mouton. All of these writers began to emphasize the apparent advantages of participative management over more traditional authoritarian approaches. Managers who were exposed to these authors and saw themselves as Theory X, or 1,1, or System 1, began to ask, "How can I change myself and my organization in the direction of Theory Y, or 9,9, or System 4?"

The methodology that was available at the time to help in that transformation was the training group, variously called the T-group, sensitivity group, encounter group, or basic group. The purposes of such group training were to help participants examine group processes, experience group problem solving, openly share information, establish a highly cohesive group climate, and build norms of shared and collaborative action. These group-centered processes, developed usually in groups of strangers with a strong focus on examination of "here and now" activity, resulted in sharing a good deal of feedback as to how group members experienced each other.

Problems in the "Family Group"

The T-group methodology was transferred into the organizational setting as the most effective method practitioners knew at the time for implementing the ideas of participative management, and for changing a work unit from System 1 or Theory X to System 4 or Theory Y. Unfortunately, the T-group method that was so successful in stranger groups had mixed results when used with "family" groups — groups composed of persons who had worked together for years in the same department. Two major problems occurred: (1) The T-group with strangers assumed a vacuum of past experience; hence, the focus on what was happening right now was most appropriate. Work groups had a long history of associations and activities. T-group trainers were not sure what areas to explore and what to leave alone. (2) T-groups disbanded and never met again, while the work unit continued intact after the sessions and people had to continue to be responsible for issues raised in the group.

Harvey and Davis identify nine more differences between the T-group in a laboratory organization and the nonlaboratory or work unit.[1]

1. Participants in laboratories are similar in personality structure. Their value systems are essentially congruent with the values of laboratory training and laboratory trainers. Persons from nonlaboratory organizations tend to have much more diverse, or at least different, personality structures.

2. Laboratories are temporary systems. Nonlaboratory or-

---

[1] Jerry B. Harvey and Sheldon A. Davis, "Some Differences between Laboratory and Non-Laboratory Organizations," in W. G. Dyer, ed., *Modern Theory and Method in Group Training* (New York: Van Nostrand Reinhold, 1972).

ganizations tend to have continuity and long-term existence.
3. In the laboratory, the problem is to build an organization. In other organizations, the problem usually is to
change existing organizational systems.
4. Laboratories are social systems. Nonlaboratory organizations are sociotechnical systems.
5. Laboratories are oriented toward the individual and
small groups. Nonlaboratory units are oriented toward
the larger organization.
6. Laboratory trainers are line managers. Organization
consultants are staff persons.
7. Laboratory organizations provide rewards that are essentially intrinsic in character. Nonlaboratory organizations tend to provide rewards that are extrinsic.
8. Data are more readily available in laboratory organizations than in nonlaboratory organizations.
9. Feedback is more readily available and less equivocal in
laboratory than in nonlaboratory organizations.

As practitioners developed more experience in applying the
T-group methods to work units, the T-group mode shifted to take
into account the differences of the new setting. It became clear
that the need was not just to let people get feedback, but to help
the work unit develop into a more effective, collaborative, problem-solving unit with work to get out and goals to achieve. Slowly
the methodology shifted from the unstructured T-group to a more
focused, defined process of training a group of interdependent
people in collaborative work and problem-solving procedures.

From Social Interactions to Task Processes

Perhaps the most significant change in the entire team-
building concept has been the increased emphasis on helping
teams achieve results: get work done. There was so much attention paid in the early stages to the relationships between people
that work matters were often neglected. Now in a team-building
program, most team facilitators and managers will make sure that
the team looks both ways: how people are working together and

how work is getting done. Both social processes and task processes are important to team success.

Team facilitators and work unit managers need to be in agreement on the focus of the team-building effort. Richard Beckhard has stated the issue this way:

> In recent years I have observed a number of team development efforts and have lately come to the realization that there may well be a discrepancy in terms of priorities between those in charge of teams engaging in such efforts and those who are facilitating them. Team leaders often see their problems as one of improving work, setting priorities, or solving problems. Consultants, trainers, and helpers often see the prime purpose as improving the workings of the group and/or the relationships of its members.[2]

Beckhard makes a strong case that the team leader, consultant, and members need to agree on what the top priority items are for the team to address. Almost all teams must do the following:

- Set goals or priorities
- Analyze or allocate the way work is performed
- Examine the way a group is working, its processes such as norms, decision making, communications
- Examine the relationships among the people doing the work

The ranking of these tasks should be agreed on by all who are involved. Clearly team building has moved beyond simply looking at the relationships between individuals and giving people feedback.

Understanding Team Variation

Anyone who has spent any time at all in different kinds of organizations is quick to recognize that all organizational teams are not alike. Certainly all have some characteristics in common;

---

[2]R. Beckhard, "Optimizing Team Building Efforts," unpublished manuscript.

they all have team members, some form of leadership or management, some identified goals, and some kind of procedure or path to achieve these goals. But along a number of other dimensions, teams may display marked differences. Current team-building theory and method takes these differences into account much more than in earlier years, when it was felt that all team processes were much the same.

Teamwork

Although all teams represent a collection of people who must collaborate, *to some degree*, to achieve common goals, there is a difference in the amount of collaboration required. Figure 3–1 represents a continuum of teamwork or collaboration needed for a team to function.

There are some teams that are not required by the nature of the task to work closely together all the time. A golf team may do some general strategy planning and share information, but in the final analysis play is by the individual performer.

An academic department also requires relatively little teamwork. Each professor can do most of the required work alone — teach, research, write. There are times when important decisions are made, and goals set that require the coordinated efforts of all department members. However, these times occur at fairly well spaced intervals.

Unlike the low teams, there are others who must meet together more regularly and whose work requires more consistent coordination. An accounting or financial department in a company would be an example. All who work must show a common accounting framework, and the work of one part of the account-

Figure 3–1
Continuum of Teamwork

Low teamwork		Average teamwork		High teamwork	
1 2	3	4 5		6 7	
Golf Team		Baseball Team		Basketball Team	
University Dept.		Accounting Dept.		NASA Space Team	
				SWAT Team	

ing financial process depends on the work of other parts. The accuracy of the tax people depends in part how well internal auditors have done their work. While each accountant may be doing individual work, there are times one may not be able to proceed without input from others.

Most company executive committees require an average amount of teamwork. For much of their work, the heads of marketing, finance, personnel, and manufacturing can work autonomously in their own areas. But at key times they must come together and build a common strategy, set common goals, and work out certain conditions such as getting marketing and manufacturing to agree on the type and amount of product that should be produced for the marketplace.

A baseball team is an example of an average teamwork situation. All nine players must be on the field at once, but for most part of the game the effort is individual in nature. Each player bats, runs, and fields alone; only the catcher and pitcher interact constantly and a few others must rely on each other in a double play or infield out.

In some groups constant teamwork is required by the nature of the task. A basketball team is on the court all together, all of the time. All members must do everything — run, shoot, play defense. Every member interacts with every other member. One would predict that a basketball team would suffer more from the lack of teamwork than would a golf or track team.

When an Air Force bomber flies a mission, every member of the crew has a specific set of assignments that are critical if the venture is to be successful. Every person depends on everyone else. Such would also be the case in a police SWAT team or the team of people in a hospital operating room. All of the tasks are highly connected and members cannot do their respective work without others doing theirs.

Variations in Team Size

Teams vary in size; some have as many as twenty people and others may be a group of three or four or even two. The dynamics of the small team of three or four are very different from the dynamics of a group of ten. In the larger organization team, the focus of the team will rarely be on all members at a particular time. When the team meets in a staff meeting, the interaction will shift from member to member and subgroup to subgroup. In the small team, the actions of each member are visible and have an impact all of the time. One can hide or coast for a time in the larger team, but if any one member tries to coast it is immediately noted in the small unit. As a result, the processes in team building with the small group are going to be different. Consider the following actual team-building case.

Team Building with the Small Team

John Clark had been a facilitator in a number of team-building sessions before, but his current assignment was a totally different experience. John found himself working with a team of three people: Ed, the project manager, and his two assistants, Gordon and Lee. Ed had called and asked John to function as the facilitator in a team-building session for the threesome. Now John found himself starting a two-and-a-half-day session and he wondered if the group would be able to handle it. What if one of the three wouldn't talk? What if the two assistants ganged up on the boss, or the boss and one of them coalesced against the other?

John and Ed had planned the start of the session. Ed began: "I wanted to spend this time working on building the three of us into a better team. From my perspective, we are not really working well together and, if you agree, I want to discover why not and what we can do about it." Ed then asked, "How well do you two think the three of us have been working together? Is there anything we can do to make our work more effective?"

John Clark observed that Gordon, one assistant, began to talk immediately. He outlined the problems as he saw them and then described the corrective actions he felt needed to be taken. Lee had not talked at all. John asked him how he saw the situation. Reluctantly Lee began to share his impressions. This pattern continued for most of the first day, with Ed asking questions, Gordon responding immediately, and Lee reluctantly coming in when asked. Finally John pointed out this recurring pattern and asked if this was usual in their meetings. They all admitted that it was. John then asked Lee if there was some reason he always talked last and reluctantly. This led to the first in-depth discussion of the dynamics of the interaction between the two. Lee pointed out two things. First, when he felt anxious or frustrated he tended to keep very quiet. Moreover, he felt that if he said something rash, Gordon would hold it against him later on. "So," said Lee, "I feel the safest way to interact with Gordon is to play it safe and not expose my hand."

Gordon was very surprised at the feedback. He talked about his tendencies to talk a lot if he was unsure. Talking helped him put his ideas into some perspective. When Lee was quiet, Gordon felt more pressure to keep talking and to try to get a resolution of the issues. It was a vicious circle: The more Gordon talked, the quieter Lee became, which caused Gordon to talk more and Lee to withdraw more — and on and on.

John then looked at Ed's role in all of this. Ed said he didn't like to come in and say anything for it might appear he was favoring one or the other. The other two felt Ed was either afraid to say anything or didn't know enough to get involved. This led both of them to lose respect for Ed.

When all of this information was on the table, the three were then able to work out a process for dealing with issues and making decisions agreeable to all.

While this small group represents a particular situation where group differences must be understood in handling a team-building session, so it will be with each unique team. Each will have its own particular patterns, history, structure, and culture that will have to be understood and taken into account in the team-building process.

New Variations of Team-Building Applications

Since organizations face a variety of new issues, structures, styles, and cultures, team building has moved to a point that a whole new range of team-building procedures are being used.

In my own work I have seen team building used successfully in several situations.

- Short, stand-up team meetings at the beginning of each day or each shift. These meetings may last for just a few minutes, but it gives the team a chance to ask such questions as these: Do we all understand the task for the day? Does anyone have any problems? Who may need some specific help? Although the time is short, the processes focus on helping the team get started correctly for the day.
- Start-up meetings for temporary task forces or project teams established for short durations.
- "Huddle" groups. These are quickly called sessions to deal with an emergency or a newly received problem or assignment. It is important to get the team's input and concurrence on actions to be taken.
- Newly formed semiautonomous work teams. This is an expanding new idea put into practice in a number of organizations when the work team has great autonomy in its actions and needs some type of team development training or skills.
- Jay Galbraith[3] makes a strong case that team development is a viable alternative in redesigning organizations. If an organization is experiencing work overload, decision-making difficulties, problems in lateral relationships, or problems in information flow and scheduling, there are a variety of redesign possibilities, but creating new teams or task forces or building up poor performing units is certainly an important method in improving the organization.

Team-building activities began to increase rapidly during the latter part of the 1960s and early 1970s. Many managers pushed to have team-development programs introduced into their organizations without critically analyzing whether or not this methodology was appropriate for their situation. In the next section we consider how to determine if a team-development program would be useful in an organization seeking change.

---

[3]Jay Galbraith, *Designing Complex Organizations* (Reading, Mass.: Addison-Wesley, 1973), ch. 6.

Part II
Preparing a Team-Building Program

4

Is Team Building Needed?

Making a Diagnosis

Before any organizational unit begins a team-development program, a thorough examination should be made so as to diagnose the nature of the team's problems. This will help determine what changes are needed and whether team building is an appropriate activity. Following are two actual cases showing the conditions that lead to using team development.

Case A: The HLW Department

The HLW Department is an agency of a state government. It has a central office in the capital city and a series of district offices throughout the state. The agency employs about 500 people and is headed by an executive director who has twelve department heads reporting to her. Through the years, the agency has been seen by similar agencies and by the people in the department as doing an effective job despite difficult circumstances.

The decision to institute some type of training or development was made initially by the training and development officer and his assistant. They were reviewing their training budget and were very much aware that approximately $5000 of unexpended funds remained in the year's budget with less than six months to go. They knew the training budget might be cut if unused funds were returned to the general fund, and that questions would be raised about the effectiveness of the training department if funds allocated for a planned program were not used.

The two considered several alternatives. First, they rejected the idea of returning unspent funds. This left them with the alternative of spending the funds. But what type of expenditure would make sense and make a contribution to the department? The assistant commented, "I recently read a good article on organization development. In my opinion, we need some OD work done in our agency."

The training director replied, "That sounds good to me, but how do you get OD started in an organization?"

"From what I read, one of the best ways is to do some team building."

"What's that?" asked the director.

"My understanding is that people who have to work together should learn how to communicate and to solve their problems so they stay solved," said the assistant. "And that sounds to me like something our executive committee [the executive director and twelve department heads] could really use."

"You can say that again," responded the training director. "But how can we sell that group on a team-building program?"

The assistant thought for a moment. "I think they would go for this program if we could get a good outside consultant to come in and conduct the program for the executive committee. An outside person would be a strong selling point to the committee."

"Agreed," said the training and development director. "Let's see if we can line up a good outside person. You get a reprint of that article on OD and we'll circulate that to the executive committee. If we can get the consultant and can set up a time and place for the team-development program that suits everyone, I think we will be in business." The OD article was circulated to all relevant poeple, two possible consultants were identified, and a meeting was set up with the executive director. They reviewed the plans with the director.

Her response was favorable. "It all looks pretty good. I think we should go ahead. My own schedule is very tight and I may not be able to stay the whole time, but I can be there to start it out and then I may have to duck out to attend some meetings in Washington. If you have a good outside person, I'm sure the whole thing will move along."

"That's my feeling," said the training director. "A good consultant will make a big difference."

So the plans were developed. A consultant was hired who had impressive credentials, and his resume was circulated to the committee. Reservations were made at an attractive resort for three days. The consultant indicated that he would like to interview people for a couple of days prior to the program, and that was agreed on. The executive director raised the team-development issue with the committee. Several people commented that they were "awfully busy," but the executive director was able to overcome these objections by pointing out that "certainly no one could disagree that it is critically important that this group become as effective a team as possible." With that, the motion to move ahead with the team-development program was unanimously approved.

Case B: The R&D Department

Tom Haymond, manager of the research and development department of the chemicals division of a large manufacturing company, had just returned from a management training program. It had been an intense five days and he had heard some things about his own management style and strategy that bothered him. Tom knew things were not going very well in his department. Because of that, he had contacted the training office and asked them to recommend a good management development course. Maybe he could get some new ideas that would be helpful. The training office had directed him to a well-known program that had a strong laboratory-training-group focus and Tom made arrangements to attend.

The week's activity had been a real eye-opener for Tom. The seven other people in his group had given him a lot of feedback about the way he tried to handle things in the group, and there were a lot of comments when he described how he ran his department back home. Tom knew he was a hard-driving, results-oriented person; he couldn't stand to see anyone or anything just sitting around. The group members at the conference told him that his insistence that the group get organized and moving had really antagonized them, and some had deliberately tried to block his efforts. One member commented that she would certainly not like to work under Tom if Tom were the same way back home as he was when the group started. Tom was quite sure he was the same way back home. That's what bothered him.

Tom had talked with his group facilitator before he left and got an agreement that if Tom wanted to do something in his own department, the facilitator would be available to help as an outside resource person.

After returning home from the conference, Tom spent part of several days planning a strategy. Finally he was ready to take action. He called an extended staff meeting for all of the section heads and project directors who reported to him, a group of ten. At the staff meeting, Tom outlined the following issues and concerns:

First he described the conditions in the department that had led him to attend the training course. The number of new developments was down, some key people had recently quit or asked for transfers; in one exit interview the terminating person had placed the reason for leaving on Tom's ineffective management behavior. Last, the attendance and participation at staff meetings was low.

Tom summarized the feedback given him at the management program. He admitted his concern about the feedback and his fear that his behavior at work was similar to that displayed during the conference. He felt that if he were to get feedback from the work group, it would be similar.

Tom then pointed out the dilemma for him. On the one hand he wanted to improve the performance level of the research and development department, but, on the other hand, he had some information that indicated he himself might be contributing to low performance. Without clear feedback both from them to him and from him to them, they might not get the basic problems identified. A plan of action for improving the situation was badly needed.

Tom asked for their suggestions. "What can I do and what can you do to help us all work on the problems that I have identified?" There was a long silence. One project head said, "I don't think things are as bad as you paint them, Tom. In my book, you're a pretty good manager." There were nods of agreement and someone said, "Right on!"

Tom replied, "I appreciate your support, but I think we would all have to agree that this department has not been as effective recently as it was two years ago. Something has happened and I'd like to find out what that is and remedy it.

"I would like to make a suggestion. I propose that we spend two or three days away from the office looking intensively at the issues I have raised today. Each person would then come prepared to give his or her own information — what basic problems affect each of us personally on the job, what causes these problems, and what we might do about them. If we put all of our information together, we might come up with some interesting new solutions.

"Also, I would like to recommend bringing in an outside resource person to help us during the two-to-three-day meeting. This person could watch us work and see if anything in my actions or the way we work together might need improving. What do you think?"

The staff began to discuss the proposal at length and, after wrestling with the issues presented, the group agreed both to go ahead with the meeting (it would start Wednesday evening and finish Friday afternoon) and to bring in an outside resource person.

Case A and Case B Considered

When we examine these two cases, it is obvious that the motivations for beginning a team-development program are quite different for the two organizations. The HLW Department needs to maintain its budget and its image. There is little enthusiasm from the executive director, but she uses her influence to "sell" the program to the executive committee. They all go along, but one could predict that when the executive director leaves after the first day, the effectiveness of action will drop. The outside consultant has inadvertently allowed his reputation to be the selling point for the program. The data suggest that the people are generally satisfied with the current performance. There is nothing in the diagnosis to suggest commitment to or — more important — a *need* for team building. One would predict — accurately as it turned out — that the team-development program would have little chance for making any real difference in how that group works together.

Case B is quite different. Most of the elements necessary for a positive team-development effort are present. The diagnosis shows that the manager has a high level of commitment to the program. He had involved his staff members early in the problem and enlisted their participation in the decision to go ahead. The boss has some insights already about his possible role in lower performance. This prepares him for negative information that may come. It will not be such a shock for people to present sensitive data or for him to hear it. The role of the outside person has been identified. The burden of the program is not on the consultant; rather, the main action is with the team. The resource program is an outside helper, not the one directing the effort. It would be expected that the program would have a good chance of leading to some action steps that make a difference, and, in fact, it did.

Diagnosing the Organization's Need for Team Development

Team development should begin with a strongly felt need to improve some basic condition or process that is interfering with the achievement of organizational goals. An organization, simply defined, is the arrangement and use of resources (human, financial, and material) to accomplish goals. Sometime in the life of almost all organizations comes a point when its members are faced with two disturbing conditions that demand change: one involves consequences or *outputs* of the organization, and the other involves *processes* or *dynamics*. When either of these begins to falter, change must be considered. It is important to observe these conditions in order to make an initial diagnosis for team building.

Organizational Outputs

All organizations, by definition, are goal oriented. When the goals, which are the ultimate achievement or output of the system, are not achieved to an adequate or satisfying degree, concern for change emerges. In our current economic system, all businesses are profit oriented. When the profit margin falls below the level defined as adequate, pressures for change result. Since profits are related to attendant conditions, such as production, sales, quality, service, labor turnover, and markets, then these conditions must be examined and changes planned. In Case B described earlier, there is some evidence that the number of new suggestions, products, and developments has declined over the past two years in the R&D department. This has led Haymond, the R&D manager, to want to begin some action, even though he is not sure of the cause of the lower productivity.

If the organization is service oriented, such as a school, church, hospital, or government agency, and the level of customer utilization of service drops below some desired level, then someone begins to plan for change. No organization can (or perhaps even should) continue to exist if it cannot maintain itself at some adequate level of organizational output or goal achievement. Pressures to change something emerge with failing outputs, and it is generally the function of management to plan and take some action to minimize or reverse these negative or undesired outputs. A critical part of any manager's job is to plan a strategy to reverse negative outputs. The organization in Case A is a service organization, but there is no indication that the outputs of the agency have fallen below the level of management satisfaction. There is little felt need to engage in a program of change.

In diagnosing an organization's outputs, it is important to review carefully all reports that show production, costs, quality, or amount of service. In addition, managers should be observing people in action and talking with them about work accomplishment.

Organizational Processes

Within every organization, there is also some standard of acceptable process, dynamics, or means by which the organization's outputs are achieved. This is sometimes referred to as group morale, the prevailing attitude about the work environment. When conditions drop below this standard, be it a formal or informal one, managers also begin to plan for change. Concern for change stems from two sources: (1) if processes or morale drop too low, the organizational outputs may be affected; and (2) if processes are too disrupted, the organization as a medium of human activity becomes too dissatisfying and the desire to improve the quality of life prompts change.

For example, almost no one enjoys working in a system where employees are subjected to constant criticism, isolation, conflict, alienation, overcontrol, and experience feelings of futility, frustration, and lack of fulfillment. It is unlikely that any organization beset with these woes could maintain its output over the long haul; but even disregarding the outputs, most modern managers would feel a responsibility for improving the general quality of life of human beings in the system. They know that poor morale can lead to labor turnover, transfers, and absenteeism. Tom Haymond has been given some feedback that suggests to him that he may be overcontrolling the work life of people under him. He wants to find out how his employees feel about his managerial behavior. Currently in the management literature much is being written about MBWA — managing by wandering around. It is through this direct interaction that much of the diagnosis about work processes and morale is made.

If the standard of acceptable processes has been objectified, then high grievance rates, turnover rates, absenteeism, complaints, transfer requests, and early retirements serve as indicators that something in the organizational dynamics and processes is not functioning adequately — and, again, someone in management needs to plan some changes somewhere. Even where objective measures are not used, most managers are sensitive to climate factors, conflicts, hostilities, or disruptions that occur in their departments, and these, too, signal that something needs to be done to improve conditions. While the R&D division has both output and process problems, the state agency appears content at both levels.

Identifying Problems

Usually a team-building program begins when a certain concern, problem, issue, or set of symptoms leads the manager to believe that the effectiveness of the staff or work unit is not up to par. Below is a list of major symptoms or conditions that usually provoke serious thought of remedial action.

- Loss of production or unit output
- Increase of grievances or complaints from the staff
- Evidence of conflicts or hostility among staff members
- Confusion about assignments, missed signals, and unclear relationships
- Decisions misunderstood or not carried through properly
- Apathy and general lack of interest or involvement of staff members
- Lack of initiation, imagination, innovation — routine actions taken for solving complex problems
- Ineffective staff meetings, low participation, minimal effective decisions
- Start up of a new group that needs to develop quickly into a working team
- High dependency or negative reactions to the manager
- Complaints from users or customers about quality of service
- Continued unaccounted increase of costs

Of this list of symptoms, most are *consequence* symptoms; that is, they result from or are caused by other factors. Loss of production is *caused* by such factors as conflicts between members or problems with one's boss. It is important to understand two causal factors.

1. *Difficulty between team members and the team leader.* This is one of the most obvious symptoms — at least it is obvious to the subordinates on the team and to an outside observer. Un-

fortunately, it may not be so apparent to the team leader. The problem is not that boss and subordinates differ, but how they deal with their differences. One common consequence of these differences is a condition of overconformity. Subordinates feel the best way to get along with the boss is to just go along with what they are told to do. They find the easiest way to manage a relationship with the superior is to fall in line. This is less stressful than to be in conflict all of the time.

At times this may represent real acceptance of the boss's position. The boss may have surrounded herself with people who are dependent, thus eliminating any possible conflict (but also eliminating the richness of diverse opinion), or the subordinates may have learned over time that conformity is the best strategy and may now automatically go along with whatever the boss suggests.

On the other hand, there is conformity that is passively resistant. People may agree with the boss publicly but privately resent and resist; there are subtle forms of resistance as decisions get lost or are never fully implemented.

The opposite of overconformity is overt resistance — openly fighting or resisting what the boss wants. Ordinary problem-solving procedures have been abandoned and whenever boss and subordinates get together there is a struggle. Here again, the struggle may go underground and while the surface interaction may seem compatible, there is heavy infighting going on behind the scenes.

It has been observed that some superiors try to manage subordinates and the possibility of resistance by assuming a very strong authoritarian stance. The authoritarian leader demands obedience and uses a variety of control methods, both formal and informal, to influence behavior. Those who are threatened by authority or who are used to high controls tend to become conforming, while those who do not accept authoritarian processes become resistant either openly or under cover.

Other difficulties between boss and subordinates arise because of a lack of trust of the boss by subordinates. Subordinates may not trust the boss to give them honest information, or to represent them honestly, or to keep confidences, or to do what was promised. When trust is low, subordinates try to protect themselves; they are very guarded in what they say and are very suspicious of decisions and promises of action.

A study by the Center of Creative Leadership showed the following reasons why executives who fail get derailed in their management careers.[1]

Reasons for Failure of Top Managers

1. Insensitivity to others — abrasive intimidating
2. Coldness, aloofness, arrogance
3. Betrayal of trust — failure to meet commitments
4. Overambitiousness — playing politics, pushing too hard to get ahead
5. Failure to handle specific performance problems — does not admit the problem, covers up, or shifts blame
6. Overmanaging — inability to delegate or build a team
7. Inability to select and develop an effective staff
8. Inability to think broadly or strategically
9. Inability to adapt to a superior with a different style
10. Overdependence on superior or mentor

The list is ranked approximately in terms of importance. Betrayal of trust is a very high item, but almost all of the top items represent behaviors that are almost antithetical to team-building behaviors. If a supervisor is insensitive, arrogant, overly ambitious, won't admit problems, or overmanages, it is very difficult for subordinates to coalesce behind the leader and build an effective team. Chapter 12 (Special Problems in Team Building) does give some suggestions for handling the situation when the boss is the major problem.

2. *Difficulty between team members.* This is one of the most widely observed symptoms of a sick team. These difficulties are described in different ways: people fight all of the time, they don't like each other, there are personality conflicts, they have different philosophies, goals, or values.

Usually the signals of team member problems are strong statements of disagreement with no attempt to reach agreements,

[1]W. McCall and R. Lombardo, "What Makes a Top Executive," *Psychology Today,* February 1983.

complaints to the boss indicating an unwillingness or inability
to work out differences, avoidance of each other except when absolutely required to interact, missed meetings or deadlines and
poor quality work, building of cliques or subgroups to protect
against the other side, minimal or very guarded communications.

It was differences in this area that originally led to the use
of group methods to surface problems between members and to
learn to work through differences.

Usually it is the manager who identifies one or more of the
above consequence or causal factors, although any unit member
may share personal observations and diagnosis. Figure 4–1 is a

Figure 4–1
Team-Building Checklist

I. Problem identification: To what extent is there evidence of the following problems in your work unit?

	Low Evidence		Some Evidence	High Evidence	
1. Loss of production or work unit output	1	2	3	4	5
2. Grievances or complaints within the work unit	1	2	3	4	5
3. Conflicts or hostility between unit members	1	2	3	4	5
4. Confusion about assignments or unclear relationships between people	1	2	3	4	5
5. Lack of clear goals, or low commitment to goals	1	2	3	4	5
6. Apathy or general lack of interest or involvement of unit members	1	2	3	4	5
7. Lack of innovation, risk taking, imagination, or taking initiative	1	2	3	4	5
8. Ineffective staff meetings	1	2	3	4	5

Figure 4–1 (*cont.*)

	Low Evidence		Some Evidence	High Evidence	
9. Problems in working with the boss	1	2	3	4	5
10. Poor communications: people afraid to speak up, not listening to each other, or not talking together	1	2	3	4	5
11. Lack of trust between boss and member or between members	1	2	3	4	5
12. Decisions made that people do not understand or agree with	1	2	3	4	5
13. People feel that good work is not recognized or rewarded	1	2	3	4	5
14. People are not encouraged to work together in better team effort	1	2	3	4	5

Scoring: Add up the score for the fourteen items. If your score is between 14 and 28, there is little evidence your unit needs team building. If your score is between 29 and 42, there is some evidence, but no immediate pressure, unless two or three items are very high. If your score is between 43 and 56, you should seriously think about planning the team-building program. If your score is over 56, then building should be a top priority item for your work unit.

II. Are you (or your manager) prepared to start a team-building program? Consider the following statements. To what extent do they apply to you or your department?

	Low		Medium	High	
1. You are comfortable in sharing organizational leadership and decision making with subordinates and prefer to work in a participative atmosphere.	1	2	3	4	5
2. You see a high degree of interdependence as necessary among functions and workers in order to achieve your goals.	1	2	3	4	5

(cont.)

Figure 4–1 (*cont.*)

	Low		Medium		High
3. The external environment is highly variable and/or changing rapidly and you need the best thinking of all your staff to plan against these conditions.	1	2	3	4	5
4. You feel you need the input of your staff to plan major changes or develop new operating policies and procedures.	1	2	3	4	5
5. You feel that broad consultation among your people as a group in goals, decisions, and problems is necessary on a continuing basis.	1	2	3	4	5
6. Members of your management team are (or can become) compatible with each other and are able to create a collaborative rather than a competitive environment.	1	2	3	4	5
7. Members of your team are located close enough to meet together as needed.	1	2	3	4	5
8. You feel you need to rely on the ability and willingness of subordinates to resolve critical operating problems directly and in the best interest of the company or organization.	1	2	3	4	5
9. Formal communication channels are not sufficient for the timely exchange of essential information, views, and decisions among your team members.	1	2	3	4	5
10. Organization adaptation requires the use of such devices as project management, task forces, and/or ad hoc problem-solving groups to augment conventional organization structure.	1	2	3	4	5
11. You feel it is important to surface and deal with critical, albeit	1	2	3	4	5

Figure 4–1 (*cont.*)

	Low	Medium	High
sensitive, issues that exist in your team.			
12. You are prepared to look at your own role and performance with your team.	1 2	3	4 5
13. You feel there are operating or interpersonal problems that have remained unsolved too long and need the input from all group members.	1 2	3	4 5
14. You need an opportunity to meet with your people and set goals and develop commitment to these goals.	1 2	3	4 5

Scoring: If your total score is between 50 and 70, you are probably ready to go ahead with the team-building program. If your score is between 35 and 59, you should probably talk the situation over with your team and others to see what would need to be done to get ready for team building. If your score is between 14 and 34, you are probably not prepared at the present time to start team building.

III. Should you use an outside consultant to help in team building? (Circle appropriate response.)

1. Does the manager feel comfortable in trying out something new and different with the staff?	Yes	No	?
2. Is the staff used to spending time in an outside location working on different issues of concern to the work unit?	Yes	No	?
3. Will group members speak up and give honest data?	Yes	No	?
4. Does your group generally work together without a lot of conflict or apathy?	Yes	No	?
5. Are you reasonably sure that the boss is not a major source of difficulty?	Yes	No	?
6. Is there a high commitment by the boss and unit members to achieve more effective team functioning?	Yes	No	?

(*cont.*)

Figure 4–1 *(cont.)*

---

7. Is the personal style of the boss and   Yes   No   ?
his or her management philosophy
consistent with a team approach?

8. Do you feel you know enough about   Yes   No   ?
team building to begin a program
without help?

9. Would your staff feel confident   Yes   No   ?
enough to begin a team-building pro-
gram without outside help?

Scoring: If you have circled six or more "yes" responses, you probably
do not need an outside consultant. If you have four or more "no" responses, you probably do need a consultant. If you have a mixture of yes,
no, and ? responses, you should probably invite in a consultant to talk
over the situation and make a joint decision.

---

checklist for identifying whether or not a team-development program is needed and whether the organization is ready to begin
such a program. In Case B, we can see that Haymond is aware of
several of these conditions in his own department. This awareness triggers the change action. Another method of making a diagnosis is to have all members of the work unit fill out the first
team-building checklist and see if they feel that problems exist
that would lead to a team-building program.

Team Development as a Change Strategy

When a unit of human beings joined together to reach goals
finds that it no longer has the capability to solve its problems well
or reach its goals at an acceptable level, it may need to look for
a way to reshape itself. Team development is one process for revitalizing a social system. When the diagnosis that results from
adequate data gathering indicates that the work unit no longer is
functioning productively, a team-development program may be
advisable as a strategy to improve effectiveness. In Case B, Tom
Haymond has enough initial data to go to his work group and
suggest a team-development program.

The underlying reason for starting a team-development program is an important factor to consider. A program should not begin unless there is clear evidence that a lack of effective teamwork is the fundamental problem. If the problem is an intergroup issue, a technical difficulty, or an administrative foul-up, team building would not be an appropriate change strategy.

5

Planning the Initial Team-Building Program

It is vital to the success of a team-development program that it be the result of a good diagnosis of the needs of the work team; depending on the need, different team-development designs may be appropriate. It would, for example, make little sense to conduct a team-development program designed to improve trust and communications if the problem is a lack of clarity of job assignments or one of general apathy and lack of innovation and energy.

Since correct diagnosis depends on clear and accurate information about the conditions to be improved, the first step is to gather data about the conditions in the system. As indicated in the previous chapter, there may already be certain signs that something is not going well in the work group. Records may show that work output is down, grievances are up, lost time is increasing, quality of work is suffering, or the number of people requesting transfer or quitting is on the increase. Or the manager may simply become aware that more and more of his or her time is being spent in dealing with personnel problems.

These initial evidences prompt the manager, executive, or administrator to ask: Why are these negative trends occurring? What should I begin to do about them?

One underlying assumption regarding teams in organizations is that resources are available in the individuals in the work unit. They have the capability to address and deal with the two questions just posed, and the problems behind these questions, if given the time, encouragement, and freedom needed to work honestly toward solutions. Team development in its best sense is creating the opportunity for people to come together to share their concerns, their ideas, and their experiences, and to begin to work together to solve their mutual problems and achieve common goals.

Team Development as a Data-Gathering, Diagnostic, Action-Planning Process

An important perspective in planning the team-development program is to envision the activity as the beginning of a process of getting work-unit members together and involving them in a total program of problem solving and development. Data-gathering, diagnosis, and action-planning activities are the initial steps in a team-development program, with action taking and evaluation as follow-up activities. In this context, the preparations for the team-development program are very simple. The manager communicates either verbally or in written form the following:

I find certain indications that we are not achieving the kinds of personal or collective results that we would like. [Here the manager may be wise to identify such indicators.] I think we should come together and spend some time examining our own activities and begin to plan for our own improvement. I would like to start with a two-day development program. Let us all come prepared to deal with the following questions: (1) What keeps us from being as effective a unit as we could be? (2) What problems do you experience that we should work on? (3) What changes do you feel we need to make to be more effective?

With this introduction, the group members begin to make the necessary psychological and informational preparations. Generally, a team development process is going to be more effective if the following conditions are present.

Cognitive Understanding. People are usually more willing to commit themselves to expending time and energy on an activity if they clearly understand what they are doing and why they are doing it. Prior to beginning the team-development program, it would be well to spend time with the staff discussing the rationale behind team development, clarifying the activities that will be involved, agreeing on the time demands, and arriving at a commitment of all group members to participate. Since it is difficult to build a team if certain members are absent, every person who is an integral member of the team should be involved. This means they should be committed psychologically to participate and the program scheduled at times when all can be present.

Membership Attendance. Ordinarily a team-development program involves a complete working unit composed of people who report to a common superior, whose work connects them with each other, and who must have at least a minimal degree of coordination, common planning, shared goals, and shared decision making in order for them to get work done. Should secretaries or office assistants be included? This depends on the role of that person in the work of the unit. Some secretaries are pure functionaries; they do only work that is assigned. Others are an extension of their bosses and are involved in setting schedules, making decisions, and carrying out action. If everyone recognizes the person as a member whose absence would affect the results of the team effort, that person should be included.

Usually the team represents only one level of an organization — a manager and his or her subordinates. However, organizations vary greatly in their structures and operations and, in some systems, mixed levels more accurately represent the working team composition.

The number of people is also a factor to consider. A group of 25 to 30 might be difficult to manage in a design that calls for each person to clarify his or her job and expectations. However, in a design centered around identifying problems and working out solutions in subgroups, that many people could be handled without major difficulty.

A rule of thumb about who to include and how many to have would be: When in doubt — include them. It's far better to have a few more in the program than to leave someone out who feels he or she should belong or be included in the department plans.

Length and Location of Program

Team development should be thought of as an ongoing process, not as a single event. People who want to get away for a couple of days and "do team building" with the idea that they will then return to doing business as usual have an incorrect notion of the purpose of team building. The whole program is designed to alter the way an integrated unit functions together. This change is *started* at an initial meeting and continues through the next several months or years until the group really learns to function as a team.

The team-development process often starts with a block of time devoted to helping the group look at its current level of team functioning and devising more effective ways of working together. This initial data-sharing, diagnosis, and action-planning sequence takes time and should not be crammed into a couple of hours. Ideally, the members of the work group could plan to meet for at least one full day, and preferably two days, for the initial program. A common format is to meet for dinner, have an evening session, and then meet all the next day or for however long a time has been set aside.

Most team-building facilitators would prefer to have a longer block of time (up to three days) to begin a team-development program. This may not be practical in some situations and modifications must be made. Since we are thinking of team development as an ongoing process, it is possible to start with shorter amounts of time regularly scheduled over a period of several weeks. Some units have successfully conducted a program that opened with an evening meeting, followed by a two- to four-hour meeting each week for the next several weeks. Commitment to the process, regular attendance, high involvement, and good use of time are all more important than length of time.

It is customary to hold the initial team-development program away from the worksite. The argument given is that if people meet at the work location, they will find it difficult to "turn off" their day-to-day concerns in order to concentrate fully on the goals of the program. This argument is compelling, even though there is little research evidence regarding the effect of the location on learning and change. Most practitioners do prefer to have development program at a location where they can have people's full time and attention.

Use of a Consultant

A common question managers ask is, "Should I conduct the team development effort on my own or should I get an outside person to help us?" "Outside person" could mean either a consultant from outside the organization or an internal consultant who is employed by the organization but is outside the work unit planning the team-development program. (Figure 4–1 includes a check-list for assessing the need for a consultant.) Ultimately, the manager should be responsible for the development of the work team. The consultant's job is to get the process started.

The use of a consultant is generally advisable if a manager is aware of problems, feels he or she may be one of the problems facing the work unit, and is not sure exactly what to do or how to do it, but feels strongly that some positive action is necessary to pull the work group together for more effective operation.

The Roles of the Manager and the Consultant

Ultimately, the development of a work team that can regularly stop and critique itself and plan for its improvement lies in the domain of management. It is the manager's responsibility to keep a finger on the pulse of his or her own organization and plan appropriate actions if the work unit shows signs of stress, ineffectiveness, or operating difficulty.

Unfortunately, many managers have not yet been trained

to do the data gathering, diagnosis, planning, and action taking required to maintain and improve their teams. The role of the consultant is to work with the manager until the manager is capable of incorporating team-development activities as a regular part of managerial responsibilities. The manager and the consultant (either an external or internal consultant) should form their own two-person team in working through the initial team-building program, always with the following in mind: (1) the manager will be responsible for all team-building activities, although he or she may use the consultant's resources; and (2) the end result of the work of the consultant is to leave the manager capable of continuing team development without the assistance of the consultant or with minimum help.

The Team-Building Cycle

Ordinarily a team-building program will follow a cycle similar to that depicted in Figure 5–1. The whole program begins because someone recognizes a problem or problems. Either before

Figure 5–1
The Team-Building Cycle

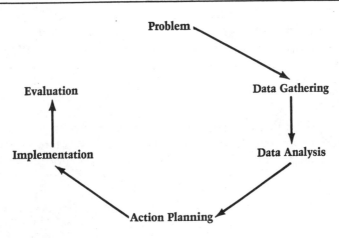

or during the team-building effort, data are gathered to determine the causes of the problem. The data are then analyzed and a diagnosis is made of what is wrong and what is causing the problem. Following the diagnosis, the work unit engages in appropriate planning and problem solving. Actions are planned and assignments made. The plans are then put into action and the results honestly evaluated. Sometimes there is no clear problem that indicates the action. The concern is then to *identify* or find the problems that are present but may be hidden. You still gather and analyze the data, identify the problems and the causes, and then move to action planning. The manager and the consultant will work together in carrying through the program from the time the problem has been identified through some form of evaluation.

Data Gathering

Since team development is essentially a program for training a staff to do its own problem solving, and since a critical condition for effective problem solving is accurate data, a major concern of the manager-consultant team is to gather clear data as to the "causes" behind the symptoms or problems originally identified. The consultant may initially assist in the data gathering, but eventually a team should develop the skill, so it can collect its own data as a basis for working on its own problems. Following are some common data-gathering devices.

Interviews. At times, the consultant can perform a useful service by interviewing the members of the staff or unit. The consultant is trying to determine the factors behind the problem(s) in order to pinpoint those conditions that may need to be changed or improved. In these interviews, the consultant will often explore the following areas: (1) Why is this unit having the kinds of problems it has? (2) What keeps you personally from being as effective as you would like to be? (3) What things do you like best about this department or unit — things you want to continue? (4) What changes would make you and this unit more effective? (5) How could this unit begin to work more effectively together as a productive team?

Following the interviews, a common practice is to have the consultant do a content analysis of the interviews, identify the major themes or suggestions that emerge, and prepare a summary presentation. At the team-building meeting the consultant would then present the summary, and the unit, under the manager's direction, would engage in analyzing the data and planning actions to deal with the major concerns.

Some consultants prefer *not* to conduct interviews prior to the team-building meeting and do not want to present a data summary. They have found that information shared in a private interview with a consultant is not as readily discussed in the open with all other team members present, especially if some of those members have been the object of some of the interview information. Consultants have painfully discovered that people often deny their own interviews, fight the data, and refuse to use it as a basis of discussion and planning. At times it may be appropriate for the consultant to interview people privately to understand some of the deep-rooted issues but still have people present their own definitions of the problems in an open session. An alternative to interviewing is open data sharing.

Open Sharing of Data. This method asks each person in the unit to share data publicly with the other group members. The data shared may not be as inclusive as that revealed in an interview, but each person feels responsible to "own up" to the information he or she presents to the group and to deal with the issue raised. To prevent forced disclosure, one good ground rule is to tell people that they should raise only those issues they feel they can honestly discuss with the others. People will generally present only the information they feel comfortable discussing; thus, the open sharing of data may result in less information, but more willingness to "work the data."

The kinds of questions suggested for the interview format are the same ones that people share openly at the beginning of the team-building session. Each presents his or her views on what keeps the unit from being as effective as it could be or suggests reasons for a particular problem. Each person also describes the things he or she likes about the unit, those things that hinder personal effectiveness, and the changes he or she feels would be helpful. All of the data are compiled on a flip chart or chalkboard. (In another variation, if the team is large, data could be gathered and shared in subgroups.) Following this, the group moves on to the next stage of the team-building cycle.

Diagnosis and Evaluation of Data

With all of the data now available, the manager and consultant must work with the group to summarize the data and put the information into a priority listing. The summary categories should be listed as either

A — those issues we can work on in this meeting

B — those issues that someone else must work (and identify who the others would be)
or

C — those issues that apparently are not open to change — things we must learn to accept or live with

Category A items become the top agenda items for the rest of the team-building session. Category B items are those where strategies must be developed for involving others. And, for category C items, the group must plan coping mechanisms. If the manager is prepared, he or she can handle the summary and the category development process. If the manager feels uneasy about this, the consultant may function as a role model to show how this is done.

The next important step is to review all of the data and to try to identify underlying factors that may be related to several problems. A careful analysis of the data may show that certain procedures, rules, or job assignments are causing several disruptive conditions.

Problem Solving and Planning

After the agenda has been developed out of the data, the roles of the manager and consultant diverge. The manager should move directly into the customary managerial role of group leader. The issues identified should become problems to solve, and plans for action should be developed.

While the manager is conducting the meeting, the consultant functions as a group observer and facilitator. Schein has referred to this activity as "process consulting,"[1] a function that others in the group can also learn to handle. In this role, the consultant helps the group look at its problem solving and work processes. He or she may stop the group if certain task or maintenance group functions are missing or being poorly performed. If the group gets bogged down or "steamrollered" into uncommitted decisions, the consultant helps look at these processes, why they occur, and how they can be avoided in the future. In this role, the consultant is training the group to develop more group problem-solving and collaborative action-taking skills.

Implementation and Evaluation

If the actions planned at the team-building session are to make any difference, they must be put into practice. This has always been a major function of management, to see that plans are implemented. The manager must be committed to the team plans; without this commitment, it is unlikely that a manager can be effective in holding people responsible for assignments agreed on in the team-building meeting.

The consultant's role is to observe the degree of action during the implementation phase and to be particularly active during the evaluation period. Another data-gathering process now begins, for that is the basis of evaluation. It is important to see if the actions planned or the goals developed during the team-building time have been achieved. This again should ultimately be the responsibility of the manager, but the consultant can be a help in training the manager to carry out good program evaluation.

The manager and the consultant should work closely together in any team-development effort. It is an ineffective program if the manager turns the whole effort over to the consultant with the plea, "You're the expert. Why don't you do it for me?" Such action leads to a great deal of dependency on the consultant, and, if the consultant is highly effective, it can cause the manager to feel inadequate or even more dependent. If the consultant is

---

[1]Edgar H. Schein, *Process Consultation* (Reading, Mass.: Addison-Wesley, 1969).

ineffective, the manager can then reject the plans developed as being unworkable or useless, and the failure of the team-building program is blamed on the consultant.

Managers should manage the enterprise. Consultants work with managers to help them plan and take action in unfamiliar areas where the manager may need to develop the skill and risk-taking attitude required to move into a new, potentially more profitable activity.

The consultant must be honest, aggressively forthright, and sensitive. He or she must be able to help the manager look at his or her own style and impact in either facilitating or hindering team effectiveness. The consultant needs to help group members get important data out in the open and keep them from feeling threatened for sharing with others. The consultant's role involves helping the group develop skills in group problem solving and planning. To do this the consultant must have a good feel for group processes and be willing to have the group look at its own dynamics. Finally, the consultant must feel a sense of pride and accomplishment when the manager and the team demonstrate their ability to solve problems independently and thus no longer need a consultant's services.

The First Team-Building Session

Perhaps the hardest hurdle to overcome in engaging in a team-development program is getting started and managing the first session. Once its process has been successfully launched, it is not too difficult to continue. It is dealing with the unknown that creates anxiety for most managers who think team building would help but have never experienced the procedure. This section will describe in detail the "getting started" activities — the typical dynamics and ways for handling them.

Step 1. Getting People's Commitment to Participate in the Team-Building Program

Most managers who start action in this area do so because they pick up signals that the work or morale in the department or unit is not as good as desired. Sometimes the unit head (supervisor or manager) has some hard data such as a report or survey that indicates some problems in the work team and this information is the stimulus for team development. However, a survey of managers who have started a team-building process indicated that three-fourths of them initiated the program because of informal signs that something was needed to increase the effectiveness of people working together. These are often such things as conflicts between people, complaints that come to the boss, or poor attendance at meetings.

When managers are willing to express their concern about the effectiveness of the team effort in the work unit and state clearly that they would like to spend time on improved teamwork, the evidence is that others in the team are usually willing to deal with this issue. The questions that are raised are usually *not* "Do we need team building," but, "What will we do? How much time will it take? Can we be sure things will get better and not worse if we engage in team building? When and where would we start the process?" and "Will we need an outside consultant or facilitator?"

In exploring the need for team building and developing commitment, the manager can do one of several things: (1) send a memo to all unit members explaining the manager's concern and feeling of need for a team-building program and ask for reactions, (2) have one-to-one interviews with each subordinate, (3) raise the issue in a unit meeting for an open discussion, (4) do either (1) or (2) and then (3).

Dealing with Resistance. In getting commitment to engage in a team-building process, one often meets resistance from one or two individuals or a subgroup. If the resistance is widespread — the manager feels team-building action is needed but others don't see the need or don't want to spend the time — it would seem that the manager and unit members are on very different wavelengths and the manager might find it useful to get an outside person to interview all members to discover what the basis of resistance is, what the real problems are, and what actions people would recommend.

Resistance by people, either one or several, usually stems from the following conditions:

- People feel that if they get into team building there will be a "bloodbath." People will be pushed into confronting others or issues that are very sensitive and things might be said or done that will be not only hurtful to individuals but harmful to the work effort.
- People may feel that they will be confronted with their own inadequate performance and they would prefer not to deal with this issue in the total group.
- They know what the major problems are in the team (a domineering boss, a personal fight between two members, restrictive policies handed down from above, too much work and too few people) and they can't see how team building is going to help.
- There is a lot of work to be done and team building will take away precious time. They can't see that the gain will be worth the time.
- They have either experienced a poor team-building effort in the past or have heard horror stories about bad experiences and their fears or fantasies conjure up all kinds of negative consequences.

Whatever the resistance factors, they must be honestly confronted or the resistance will go underground and surface during the team-building meetings or in foot dragging when it comes time to implement actions that come out of the program.

The best way to handle the resistance is to have the manager or the facilitator list the preceding common resistance factors in a preliminary meeting, describe the goals and processes of the team-building sessions, and define the limits or ground rules that would virtually prohibit destructive actions from occurring.

It must be admitted, however, that a key ingredient is the unit members' level of trust that both the manager and facilitator have the courage and skill to move into areas that need exploring but will avoid harmful criticism or confrontation. The basic ground rule is that the function of the team is to engage in problem solving — to deal with the issues in the team and to improve functioning, not to create more problems. It is established at this preliminary session that during the team-building sessions if anyone has a concern that the process is becoming dysfunctional or destructive to anyone, he or she has the right and responsibility to say, "I feel uneasy about what is going on and want to ask if this is really solving our problems."

Step 2. Establishing the Agenda

Usually people want to know what they are going to talk about in the team-building sessions. Just to tell people, "We are going to spend three days doing team building," without indicating what is going to be discussed generally will raise, not lower, their level of anxiety and concern and will reduce commitment.

There are a variety of ways the agenda for the team building can be developed so people will know in advance what to expect. (1) The manager can develop an agenda and circulate it for any additions or modifications. (2) The team can produce its own agenda at a unit meeting. (3) An outsider can interview people and make a list of common problems or issues to be discussed. Following is an actual agenda for one team-building program. The first draft of the agenda was created by the manager, then circulated to team members for their review and additions, which resulted in the final agenda.

Team-Building Agenda

1. Goals
   a. What should the goals be for the team-building session?
   b. What should the overall goals be for our unit?
   c. What should the goals be for yourself?
2. Strategic planning. Where do we want to be in 1, 3, 5 years?
3. Expectations. What do we expect of others on the team? The management? What are the manager's expectations of team members?
4. Decision making. Who makes what decisions? How should decisions be made?
5. Organization. Are we organized appropriately?
6. Morale. What is the current level of morale in our unit? How could it be improved?
7. Relations with other units. How well are we working with other departments? With headquarters?

8. Strengths and weaknesses. What do we see as our strengths as a unit? Our weaknesses? How do we correct our weaknesses?
9. Current problems. Are there any current problems or concerns not listed that we need to address?

This is only one example of the kind of agenda that could be developed for a team-building program. Remember, the issue in team building is to develop the ability for the team to identify its own problems and to solve them.

One highly experienced team had a unique method for developing its team-building agenda. The team would meet and the facilitator would say, "On the count of three, point to the person or persons you are currently having the biggest problems with. Ready: one, two, three." At this everyone would point, they would look to see who was pointing at whom, and the agenda was set.

Another team used a rather short agenda:

1. What are the biggest problems our team is currently facing?
2. What keeps our team from being as effective as it could be?
3. What actions do we need to take to solve our problems and improve our team expectations?

Step 3. Setting the Team-Building Session: Time and Place

Very little systematic research has been done to see empirically what length of sessions, location, and procedures account for best results in team building. There is a rationale for setting up initial team-building programs in the following way:

1. The first session should be for an extended block of time (two or three days).

   Rationale: It takes time to build a climate to deal with some sensitive issues. Unless you have a block of time, you are always starting over if you only have a series of short sessions. Additionally, some problems are very complex and it just takes time to get through the various aspects of them.

2. The first session should be off-site, away from the work place.

   Rationale: If people are in a conference room at work, there are too many possible distractions — phone calls, running to the office, handling day-to-day matters during lunch time or a coffee break.

It should almost go without saying that the team-building session ordinarily should not be held at a "crisis" period or extremely high pressure or busy times. If it is held during this high-intensity period, people will resent being at the session when they feel they should be back on the job.

Step 4. The First Session

Some have preferred to start the first session on a social note. They have dinner together and then the first session lasts for about two hours after dinner. The session is devoted to reviewing the agenda, looking at the goals of the team-building meeting, setting any ground rules, and assigning priorities to the agenda items so they know what issue they will begin with in the morning.

Another sequence is to start the first thing in the morning and outline the work for the total day without the social aspects of a meal before time. But whatever the starting time, the following matters need to be handled during the first session.

- Housekeeping details. Time of meetings and meals. Break time. How to handle phone calls.
- Discussion of the goals of the team-building session. An expression of commitment by the team leader.
- Introduction of and clarification of the role of the facilitator.
- Review of the agenda. Since people should have seen the agenda in advance, it should not be a surprise. They should, however, have a chance to make additions or amendments and, most important, list the agenda issues in terms of priority. This will identify those matters the team wants to work on first.

It is important that the team leader (manager) be in charge of the session. It is not the facilitator's meeting. It is a problem-solving meeting with hoped for actions and decisions forthcoming that require the directing hand of the manager to ensure follow-through.

Step 5. Teamwork at Two Levels

After the agenda has been set into a priority list, the team begins to address the agenda items. They will use whatever process or procedures are customary for them. However, it should be made clear at the outset that there will always be two levels of work — or two agendas. As the team addresses an agenda item, the facilitator (and hopefully team member) may from time to time ask the team to stop its work and to look at *how* it is doing its work. This is the role of the facilitator as a process consultant. The agenda now shifts to looking at the team's process or way of working.

It is quite possible that because the team has inadequate processes, its problems or tasks do not get solved. Teams must have a commitment to work at both levels and not feel frustrated when they move from task to process and then back again.

6

Design Options
An Overview

The overall goal of any team-development program is to improve the effectiveness of a group that must work together to achieve results. Argyris[1] has identified three conditions he feels are characteristic of a healthy or effective organization or organizational unit: (1) the ability to gather relevant data; (2) the ability to make sound, free, and informed choices or decisions; and (3) the ability to implement those decisions with commitment.

In addition to these three conditions, most professionals working with teams would identify the following factors as other characteristics of an effective team:

1. Goals are clear and understood and accepted by all team members. Nash,[2] in his review of productive actions in organizations, also says that goals must be specific and *hard*. If they are too easy they lack the ability to challenge and motivate people and if they are too hard people feel overwhelmed before they start.

---

[1]C. Argyris, *Intervention Theory and Method* (Reading, Mass.: Addison-Wesley, 1970).

[2]M. Nash, *Making People Productive* (San Francisco: Dorsey-Bass Publishers, 1985), pp. 22–27.

2. There is a climate of trust and support. In all of his work as head of the University of Michigan's Survey Research Center, the late Rensis Likert developed only one principle he felt was essential in any organization or work team. He called this the "Principle of Supportive Relationships."

> The leadership and other processes of the organization must be such as to ensure a maximum probability that in all interactions and in all relationships within the organization, each member, in light of his/her background, values, desire, and expectations, will view the experience as supportive and one which builds and maintains his/her sense of personal worth and importance.[3]

3. Differences between people are identified and worked through rather than ignored, suppressed, or allowed to build into open conflict.
4. People understand and accept their roles in the work unit and how they fit into the overall framework of both the team and the organization.

Given these characteristics, the team would set as one of its goals to maximize the development of such qualities into the team.

Another way of describing a team-building program is that its purpose is to help the work unit engage in a constant process of self-examination to gain awareness of those conditions that keep the unit from functioning effectively. Having gathered the data, the work group learns how to use the data for making decisions, and then takes those actions that will lead to a growing state of health. Team development, in this sense, is a continual, ongoing process — not a one-time activity.

Team development often begins with a block of time, usually two or three days, during which the team starts learning how to engage in its own review, analysis, planning action, making

---

[3]R. Likert, *The Human Organization* (New York: McGraw-Hill, 1967), p. 47.

decisions, and even taking action. Following the first meetings, the team may periodically take other blocks of time to continue the process, to see what progress has been made since the last team meeting and what should be done to continue to improve the overall effectiveness. It is also possible that, in time, the team will develop its skill for development to such a point that team members are continually aware of areas that need improvement and raise them at appropriate times with the appropriate people, thereby making it unnecessary to set aside a special meeting for such action.

There is no one way to put together a team-building program. The format will depend on the experience, interests, and needs of the team members, the experience and needs of the manager, the skills of the consultant (if one is needed), and the nature of the situation that has prompted the meeting.

Following are a range of design alternatives for each phase of a team-building program. Those planning such an activity may wish to select various design elements from among the alternatives that seem applicable to their own situation.

Preparation

This phase has been described in the previous chapter on planning the program and need not be reviewed in detail here. In general, the program must be well conceived and those involved must have indicated at least a minimal commitment to participate. Commitment will be increased if people understand clearly *why* the team-building program is being proposed and if they have an opportunity to influence the decision to go ahead with the program.

If this is the first time this group has ever spent some time together with the specific assignment to review their group effectiveness and to plan for change, there is likely to be a good deal of anxiety and apprehension. (Major resistance forces were discussed earlier.)

Questions of deep concern probably will not be eliminated, but may be reduced as a climate is set and as people "test the water" and find that plunging in is not all that awesome. Experience will be the best teacher and people will allay or confirm their fears as the sessions proceed. Those conducting the session may anticipate such concerns and can raise them prior to the first meeting to reduce any extreme anxiety by openly describing what will happen and what the hoped-for outcome will be.

Alternative Actions

I. Have an outside person interview each unit member to identify problems, concerns, and needs for change.

II. Invite an outside speaker to talk about the role of teams in organization and the purposes of team development.

III. Gather data on the level of team effectiveness. (See the instruments presented in this book; see also Figure 6–1.)

IV. Have a general discussion at a staff meeting about the need for a team-building program.

V. Invite in a manager who has had a successful team-building experience to describe the activities and results in his or her unit.

Goals. The goals of this phase are to explain the purpose of team building, get commitment for participation, and do preliminary work for the workshop.

Start-up Phase

During this part of a team-development workshop, people come together and begin the process of establishing a climate for work. The climate established will, of course, influence the rest of the program.

Alternative I

A. The superior can give a short opening talk, reviewing the goals as he or she sees them and the need for the program, emphasizing his or her support, and reaffirming the norm that no negative sanctions are intended for any open, honest behavior.

Figure 6–1
Team Development Scale, by William G. Dyer

1. To what extent do I feel a real part of the team?

1	2	3	4	5
Completely a part all the time	A part most of the time	On the edge, sometimes in, sometimes out	Generally outside, except for one or two short periods	On the outside, not really a part of the team

2. How safe is it in this team to be at ease, relaxed, and myself?

1	2	3	4	5
I feel perfectly safe to be myself; they won't hold mistakes against me.	I feel most people would accept me if I were completely myself, but there are some I am not sure about.	Generally, you have to be careful what you say or do in this team.	I am quite fearful about being completely myself in this team.	A person would be a fool to be himself in this team.

3. To what extent do I feel "under wraps," that is, have private thoughts, unspoken reservations, or unexpressed feelings and opinions that I have not felt comfortable bringing out into the open?

1	2	3	4	5
Almost completely under wraps	Under wraps many times	Slightly more free and expressive than under wraps	Quite free and expressive much of the time	Almost completely free and expressive

(cont.)

Figure 6-1 (cont.)

4. How effective are we, in our team, in getting out and using the ideas, opinions, and information of all team members in making decisions?

1	2	3	4	5
We don't really encourage everyone to share their ideas, opinions, and information with the team in making decisions.	Only the ideas, opinions, and information of a few members are really known and used in making decisions.	Sometimes we fear the views of most members before making decisions and sometimes we disregard most members.	A few are sometimes hesitant about sharing their opinions, but we generally have good participation in making decisions.	Everyone feels his or her ideas, opinions, and information are given a fair hearing before decisions are made.

5. To what extent are the goals the team is working toward understood and to what extent do they have meaning for you?

1	2	3	4	5
I feel extremely good about goals of our team.	I feel fairly good, but some things are not too clear or meaningful.	A few things we are doing are clear and meaningful.	Much of the activity is not clear or meaningful to me.	I really do not understand or feel involved in the goals of the team.

6. How well does the team work at its tasks?

1	2	3	4	5
Coasts, loafs, makes no progress	Makes a little progress, most members loaf	Progress is slow, spurts of effective work	Above average in progress and pace of work	Works well, achieves definite progress

7. Our planning and the way we operate as a team are largely influenced by:

1	2	3	4	5
One or two team members	A clique	Shifts from one person or clique to an...	Shared by most of the members some...	Shared by all members of the team...

Figure 6–1 (*cont.*)

8. What is the level of responsibility for work in our team?

1	2	3	4	5
Each person assumes personal responsibility for getting work done.	A majority of the members assume responsibility for getting work done.	About half assume responsibility, about half do not.	Only a few assume responsibility for getting work done.	Nobody (except perhaps one) really assumes responsibility for getting work done.

9. How are differences or conflicts handled in our team?

1	2	3	4	5
Differences or conflicts are denied, suppressed, or avoided at all cost.	Differences or conflicts are recognized, but remain unresolved mostly.	Differences or conflicts are recognized and some attempts are made to work them through by some members, often outside the team meetings.	Differences and conflicts are recognized and some attempts are made to deal with them in our team.	Differences and conflicts are recognized and the team usually is working them through satisfactorily.

10. How do people relate to the team leader, chairman, or "boss"?

1	2	3	4	5
The leader dominates the team and people are often fearful or passive.	The leader tends to control the team, although people generally agree with the leader's direction.	There is some give and take between the leader and the team members.	Team members relate easily to the leader and usually care able to influence leader decisions.	Team members respect the leader, but they work together as a unified team with everyone participating and no one dominant.

11. What suggestions do you have for improving our team functioning?

71

B. The role of the consultant, if there is one, can be explained either by the manager or the consultant.

C. Participants may fill out and share their immediate here-and-now feelings about the meetings by responding to the following questions handed out on a sheet of paper. They call out their answers (to set the norm of open sharing of data) and the person at the flipchart records:

1. How confident are you that any real change will result from these meetings?

1	2	3	4	5
Not confident at all		Some confidence		High

2. To what degree do you feel the people really want to be here and work on team-development issues?

1	2	3	4	5
Don't really want to be here		Some interest in being here		High interest in being here

3. How willing do you think people are to actually make changes that may be suggested?

1	2	3	4	5
Will be unwilling to change		Some willingness to change		Very willing to change

4. How willing do you think you and others will be to express real feelings and concerns?

1	2	3	4	5
Not very willing		Some degree of willingness		Very willing

For a group of eight people, the tabulated data, gathered and presented before the group, might look like this. The profile line is a connection of quickly estimated means.

The group of eight could then be divided into two groups of four and asked to discuss: Why is this profile rather low, and what would have to be done here to increase the positive orientation of people toward these meetings?

Subgroups then discuss for twenty minutes and report back to the total group. The purpose of this type of beginning is to set the norm that the whole program is centered on data gathering, data analysis, open sharing, and trying to plan with data. This also allows group members to test the water about here-and-now data rather than more sensitive work-group issues, to see how people will respond and react to the questions.

Alternative II

After preliminary remarks by the manager, the group members could be asked: In order for us to get a picture of how you see our group functioning, would each of you take a few minutes to describe our group as a kind of animal or combination of animals, a kind of machine, a kind of person, or whatever image comes to mind.

Some groups in the past have been described as

- A hunting dog — a pointer. We run around and locate problems, then stop and point and hope somebody else will take the action.
- A Cadillac with pedals. We look good on the outside, but there is no real power to get us moving.
- A Rube Goldberg device. Everything looks crazy and you can't imagine anything will ever happen, but, in some way, for some reason, we do get results at the end.

• An octopus. Each tentacle is out grasping anything it can but doesn't know what the other tentacles are doing.

As people share such images and explain what elicits the image, some questions may be asked: What are the common elements in these images? Do we like these images of ourselves? What do we need to do to change our image? Answering these questions becomes the major agenda item for subsequent group meetings.

A variation of the above is to have subgroups of two to four people build a collage. They are given magazines and other materials, crayons, magic markers, and a large piece of cardboard and then asked to assemble a collage representing their work unit. The collages are then displayed and explained, and questions similar to those above are asked and then used as a basis for subsequent work.

Alternative III

In this alternative, the group is asked, usually by the consultant, to work on a major decision-making problem (NASA exercise, Subarctic or Desert Survival,[4] Tinker Toy building, or the exercise *Agree-Disagree Statements on Teams* shown in Figure 6–2) and to function under the direction of the superior in a fashion similar to the way they work on problems back home. The consultant acts as a process observer. After the exercise, the consultant gets the group members to review their own processes and determine their strengths in problem solving, as well as their deficiencies. The consultant shares with the group his or her observations. Lists of positive and negative features are compiled. The agenda for the following sessions is set: How do we maximize our strengths and overcome our deficiencies? For example, if the process review indicates that the group is very dependent on the leader, that some people are overwhelmed by the "big talker," and that the group jumps to decisions before everyone has a chance to put in ideas, the agenda is how to reduce or change these negative conditions.

---

[4]See the exercises from *Experimental Learning Methods*, 39818 Plymouth Road, Plymouth, Michigan 48170.

Figure 6–2
Agree-Disagree Statements on Teams

Instructions: Read each statement once. Check whether you agree (A) or disagree (B) with each statement. Take about four minutes for this. Then in groups try to agree or disagree *unanimously* with each statement *as a group.* Try especially to discover reasons for disagreement. Try first to come to agreement as the statement is written, but if you cannot come to agreement, see if you can change the wording so all can agree.

Key: "A" if you agree; "B" if you disagree

( ) 1. A primary concern of all team members should be to establish an atmosphere where all are free to express their opinions.

( ) 2. In a team with a strong leader, an individual is able to achieve greater personal security than in a team with a more passive leader.

( ) 3. There are often occasions when an individual who is a part of a working team should do what s(he) thinks is right regardless of what the group has decided to do.

( ) 4. Members should be required to attend meetings for setting team goals and discussing team problems.

( ) 5. Generally there comes a time when democratic group methods must be abandoned in order to solve practical problems.

( ) 6. In the long run it is more important to use involvement-participative methods than to achieve specific results by other means.

( ) 7. Sometimes it is necessary to change people in the direction you yourself think is right, even when they object.

( ) 8. It is sometimes necessary to ignore the feelings of others in order to reach a group decision.

( ) 9. When leaders are doing their best, one should not openly criticize or find fault with their conduct.

( ) 10. Meetings would be more productive if the leader would get quickly to the point and say what s(he) wants the group to do.

( ) 11. By the time the average person has reached maturity, it is almost impossible for him/her to increase his/her skill in group participation.

(cont.)

Figure 6-2 *(cont.)*

( ) 12. Interest falls off when everybody in the group has to be considered before making decisions.

( ) 13. Teamwork increases when the leader is careful to choose friends as team members.

( ) 14. A team is no stronger than its weakest member.

( ) 15. In the long run, it is more productive to replace an ineffective team member than to try and retrain him/her.

( ) 16. Once a team gets established in a set way of working, it is almost impossible to change.

( ) 17. When a team gets a new leader, the whole pattern of the team changes.

( ) 18. One resistant team member can keep a whole team from improving its performance.

( ) 19. The most important condition in a successful team-building program is the motivation level of the team leader to want to see the program succeed.

( ) 20. To become a really effective team, members should have a personal liking for each other.

Goals. The goals of this phase are to create a climate for work; to get people relaxed and loosened up; to establish norms for being open, for planning, and for dealing with issues; and to present a cognitive framework for the whole experience.

Group Problem-Solving and Process-Analysis Phase

Whatever the start-up method, or combination of methods used, the next phase usually involves two parts: (1) the work unit begins to engage in the problem-solving process; and (2) a process consultant or observer helps the group to look at its skill in working on problems as an effective team, as a prelude to improving its problem-solving capabilities.

The McGregor and Likert characteristics (see Chapter 2) of an effective group become useful checklists for the group observer. The process consultant is usually trying to see to what extent the group is effective at both task activities and relationship–maintaining activities. Ineffective teams will often be characterized by such conditions as

- Domination by the leader
- Warring cliques or subgroups
- Unequal participation and uneven use of group resources
- Rigid or dysfunctional group norms and procedures
- A climate of defensiveness or fear
- Uncreative alternatives to problems
- Restricted communications
- Avoidance of differences or potential conflicts

Such conditions would reduce the team's ability to work together in collective problem-solving situations. The role of the consultant would be to help the group become aware of its processes and begin to develop greater group skills. Specifically, after becoming aware of a process problem, the group needs to establish a procedure, guideline, or plan of action to reduce the negative condition.

Alternative I

Following the opening remarks, the consultant, outside person, or manager presents data that have been collected from the group members via interviews or instruments prior to the meeting. The group is asked to analyze the data: What do the data mean? Why do we respond the way we do? What conditions give rise to negative responses? What do we need to change to get a more positive response to our own organization?

This analysis can best be done in subgroups (three to four people) and then shared and compiled into a total listing of issues and possible change actions. The summaries form the basis for the subsequent sessions. The group also puts the data into categories as described earlier. The category A items are the major work issues on the agenda.

Alternative II

This design requires some extensive case analysis prior to the team-building sessions. An external consultant, a company OD person, or someone in management pulls together from one to several case studies, vignettes, or critical incidents that seem to represent some recurring problems in the work unit. Another possibility is to have each member write up a short case that represents a problem area for him or her. Again, the group task is to look at the several cases, try to discover what the underlying conditions are that trigger such conditions, and then plan action for reducing the likelihood that such conditions would occur again.

Alternative III

In this method, objective data gathered from records in the work unit are compiled and presented to the group members. Such information as the production records, grievance rate, absenteeism, turnover, lost time, budget discrepancies, late reports, cost increases, and so on are included in this feedback. The group's job is to conduct an in-depth analysis of the data, diagnose the course of negative trends, and then engage in action planning for improvement.

Alternative IV

Instead of data from prior data-collection methods being presented to the group, data about the conditions or problems of the team are surfaced at the team meeting or in an agenda of problems or issues developed prior to the session. Each person is asked to come prepared to share his or her perception of the following: (1) What keeps this work group from functioning at its maximum potential? (2) What keeps you, personally, from doing the kind of job you would like to do? (3) What things do you like in this unit that you want to have maintained? (4) What changes would you like to see made that would help you and the whole group? Group members or the leader may have other items they would like to put on the agenda.

Group members each take a turn sharing their information. The responses are listed on newsprint and common themes are identified. The most important issues are listed in priority and they become the items for discussion.

Problem-Solving Process

Regardless of the alternative selected above, the work unit should by this point have identified a series of problems, concerns, or issues. The team next must move into a problem-solving process by engaging in the following actions:

1. Put problems in order of priority and select the five or six most pressing problems to be addressed during the workshop.
2. Begin the classic problem-solving process: Define the problem, list alternative solutions, select alternative to be implemented, work out action plan, perform the action, evaluate the results.
3. Work out forcefield analysis.[5] Identify the existing level of group effectiveness, formulate a goal, identify driving and restraining forces, develop plan to remove restraining forces.
4. Begin role negotiations. Negotiate between people or subunits the actions needed from each other to improve effectiveness.
5. Set up task-force teams or subunits. Give each team a problem to work on. Set up the actions, carry out the action, and assess the results.
6. After all problems have been listed, the group sorts them into: (a) those problems we can work on here; (b) those problems someone else must handle (and identify who that is); (c) those problems we must live with since they appear to be beyond our ability to change.
7. Set targets, objectives, or goals. The group spends time identifying short- or long-range goals it wishes to achieve, makes assignments, and sets target dates for completion.

---

[5]Kurt Lewin, "Group Decision and Social Change," in Maccoby et al., eds., *Readings in Social Psychology* (New York: Holt, 1958). See also W. G. Dyer, *Strategies for Managing Change* (Reading, Mass.: Addison-Wesley, 1984), chap. 2.

Goals. To begin to take action on the problems identified. To make assignments and set dates for the completion of work. To practice better problem-solving, decision-making, planning, objective-selecting, and delegation skills.

Interpersonal, Subunit, and Group Feedback Phase

Often, a major issue following the identification of problems is the sharing of feedback to individuals, subparts of the team, or to the work group as a whole. Certain actions, functions, or personal styles and strategies on the part of one or more people may be clogging up the teamwork and preventing achievement of goals and satisfaction for certain other team members. If such is the case, it may be legitimate to engage in an open feedback session. The goal is to share data about performance so difficulties can be resolved. It is critical that a feedback session *not* slip into name calling, personal griping, or verbal punishing of others. All feedback given should reflect a genuine willingness to work cooperatively: "My performance suffers because of some things that happen in which you are involved. Let me share my feelings and reactions so you can see what is happening to me. I would like to work out a way that we all can work more productively together."

Feedback is most helpful if it can be given in descriptive fashion, or in the form of suggestions.

Descriptive Feedback. Describes behavior or action and its impact. Example: "John, when you promise me that you will have a report ready at a certain time (as happened last Thursday) and I don't get it, that really frustrates me. It puts me behind schedule and makes me feel very resentful toward you. Are you aware that such things are going on, and how should we work out this kind of problem?"

Suggestions. "John, let me make a suggestion that would really be of help to me as we work together. If you could get your reports to me on time, particularly those that have been promised at a certain time, it would help my work schedule and reduce my frustration. Also, if I don't get a report on time, what would you prefer I do about it?"

Other Possibilities. Following are some other ways group members go about sharing feedback with one another.

1. Each person has a sheet of newsprint on the wall. Everyone writes on the sheets of others items in three areas: (a) things we want you to *begin* doing (that will increase your effectiveness); (b) things we want you to *stop* doing; and (c) things we want you to *continue* to do.
2. Envelope exchange. Each person writes a note to others covering the same issues as in item 1 and gives the notes to the others.
3. Confirmation-disconfirmation process. Group members summarize how they view themselves and their own work performance — their strengths and areas that need improvement. Others are asked to confirm or disconfirm the person's diagnosis.
4. Management profile. Each person presents the profile of his or her effectiveness from previously gathered data (from instruments like the BSR Management Profile, Telometrics Profile, and Scientific Methods Grid Profile). Group confirms or disconfirms the profile.
5. Analysis of subunits. If the team has subunits, each subunit is discussed in terms of what it does well, what it needs to change, and what it needs to improve.
6. Total unit or organizational analysis.[6] The group looks at how it has been functioning and critiques its own performance over the past year. It identifies things it has done well and areas that need improvement.
7. Open feedback session. Each person who would like feedback may ask for it in order to identify areas of personal effectiveness and areas that need improvement.
8. Prescription writing. Each person writes a prescription for others: "Here is what I would prescribe that you do

[6]Richard Beckhard, "The Confrontation Meeting," *Harvard Business Review 45* (March-April 1967): 149–155.

(or stop doing) in order to be more effective in your position." Prescriptions are then exchanged.

Goals. This phase is designed to share feedback among people in such a way as to help them improve their effectiveness and to give feedback to work units with the same objective in mind.

Action-Planning Phase

The end result of all the activities mentioned above is to help the work unit identify those conditions that are blocking both individual and group effectiveness, so that the group may begin to develop plans for action and change. Decisions for action should be made with a commitment to carry such action to completion. During this phase, plans are developed, assignments are given, procedures are outlined, and dates are set for completion and review. Often the plan is a set of agreements regarding who is willing to take a specific action. All such agreements should be written down, circulated, and followed up later to ensure they have been carried out.

Below is a set of actions that are possible during the action-planning phase:

1. Each person takes time to evaluate his or her feedback and develops a plan of action for personal improvement. This plan is presented to the others.
2. Contract negotiations.[7] If there are particular problems between individuals or subunits, specific agreements for dealing with conflict issues are drawn up and signed.
3. Assignment summary. Each person summarizes what his or her assignments are and the actions he or she intends to take as a follow-up of the team-development meeting.
4. Subunit or group plans. If development plans have been completed, such plans are presented and reviewed.

---

[7]R. Harrison, "Role Negotiations: A Tough-Minded Approach to Team Development," in W. Burke and H. Hornstein, eds., *The Social Technology of Organization Development* (Washington, D.C.: NTL Learning Resources, 1971).

5. Schedule review. The group looks at its time schedule and its action plans. Dates for completion and dates for giving progress reports on work being done are confirmed. Schedule for the next staff meeting is set. If another team-development workshop or meeting is needed, it may be scheduled at this time.

Goals. The goal of this phase is to confirm and pinpoint changes, goals, assignments, and dates for completion.

Follow-up Phase

Unless the decisions made and actions planned are actually implemented, the functioning of the team will not improve. It is important that follow-up meetings are scheduled and a review conducted of decisions and actions. The manager in charge must manage the follow-up efforts. If a good three-day team-building meeting is held, but the excitement and enthusiasm that is generated is allowed to dissipate because of a lack of follow-through, there is the danger that the level of effectiveness of the work unit will decrease and the team-building meetings will have had, in the long run, a negative effect.

In the follow-up phase, certain alternative courses of action are possible (a more extensive discussion of the follow-up process is presented in Chapter 7):

1. Process review. At the end of the workshop, time may be taken to critique the team-development program — things that went well, things that need to be changed, recommendations for the next time-development meeting, and so on.
2. Management review and follow-through. All assignments and action plans are reviewed by appropriate managers or management groups to make sure these plans are supported and reviewed, and that commitments called for at appropriate dates have been set.
3. Task forces or committees may have been formed. Specific dates are set to have these work groups report on the results of their efforts.

4. Following the initial team-building meeting, shorter periods of time may be used to have a continuation of the first team-building meeting. It may be possible to have a four-hour block to review the work done since the last meeting, gather new data, make new assignments, and plan for the next session. Team building in this manner becomes an ongoing process.

Goals. The major goals in this phase are to establish a system that will ensure that actions agreed on and agreements made are, in fact, implemented. Clear deadlines are set and the regular processes of management are followed to ensure completion. A major goal is to see that continual team building becomes a part of the ongoing activities of the work group.

Keeping in mind the many design options and alternatives we have discussed, consider the following case example of an organization that engaged in a team-development program.

Illustrative Case: WMBA and Channel 12

When the staff of a broadcast system composed of radio station WMBA and television channel 12 began a major organization improvement effort, it was the result of several months of thinking and planning. Bruce Chamberlain, the station manager, had been extremely conscious of a loss of revenues, harder times in selling television and radio spots, and evidence of a drop-off in listening and viewing publics. There were indications that the radio and TV groups were at odds with each other, program materials were not as creative as they used to be, and the sales staff seemed to be dragging its feet.

Bruce reviewed these conditions with the managers who reported to him. The total station staff fluctuated between forty and sixty people, depending on the season and workload, and was divided into the major groupings of radio, television, production, sales, personnel, finances, and smaller special groups in FM radio, special effects and projects, and public service. A managers' meeting was held each week and Chamberlain had suggested that the whole station needed to review its overall activities to see how all phases of their operations could improve. Bruce had contacted a nearby university and found a professor knowledgeable in organization development methods who had met with him and outlined a series of alternatives. Since the station management group annually got together for a retreat for business and social reasons, Bruce felt that this time could be better used to seriously review their entire organization, do some more effective planning and coordination, and iron out some of the interface problems.

This proposal was discussed at length in the managers' meeting and finally agreed on. The dates were set, location agreed on, a decision was made to hire an outside resource person, and a committee was set up to make all detailed arrangements.

The outside person met with the managers at a later meeting and outlined the purpose of such a two-day program. The managers suggested issues they would like addressed, the consultant reviewed several possible design arrangements, and it was agreed that the committee assigned (which included Chamberlain) would work with the consultant in making final program plans. Notice of the meeting was shared with all station personnel, and those who were to participate received both a verbal and written invitation. They were asked to come prepared to review the total functioning of the broadcast system and to spend time giving their suggestions for improving the entire system.

The initial session began on Wednesday evening and the program was to end at 3:00 P.M. on Friday. Following dinner, the Wednesday evening session began at 7:30. Chamberlain first outlined the need for the session as he saw it and noted some problems he hoped to address. The consultant was introduced and her role clarified — she would handle some parts of the program, present some lecture inputs, direct some activities, and be a process observer. The group was then asked to break into four subgroups, with four or five people in each group. Eighteen people had been invited to this session. This group included the key management, supervisory, and administration people who all worked quite closely together.

The subgroups were asked to think about the overall broadcasting system and to come up with an animal, vehicle, general image, or any combination of things that would best describe the organization as they saw it.

In the groups there was a lot of laughter as people came up with wild ideas. After a half hour, each group shared its images with the rest. Everyone agreed on two images.

1. The organization was like a combination dog, a pointer-setter-terrier. It would point at flaws or problems, it would sit down and wait for someone to do something, and it would yelp like a terrier if anyone did anything out of the ordinary.

2. The organization was like a kaleidoscope. Lots of beautiful images were created, but with just a slight turn the image would change. Nothing was stable or constant, but the picture always looked good to an outside observer.

Individuals were asked to do some private planning that evening and work in the small groups again in the morning. The topics: What do we do that makes us feel we have the image we think we have? What are our biggest problems as an organization? What do we need to do to alter our image and deal with our problem areas?

The next morning the small groups met for nearly two hours. When the groups came together and combined their data, the list of issues was sobering. There were several major concerns. (1) Too much time was spent trying to please the board of directors and not enough attention was being paid to the public. (2) Each area was fighting with others, trying to "build a kingdom" rather than sharing ideas and information. (3) Staff meetings were bull sessions rather than productive working periods. (4) People were trying to pad budgets and expenses. (5) Those who had to serve TV, radio, and FM in special staff capacities were not clear as to priorities, time commitments, or assignments. (6) There was a tendency to put blame for problems on someone else; nobody ever admitted any problems in one's own area. (7) A major goal was to try to look good on paper — have everything in order without being concerned about quality performance.

Together the group arranged the seven major problems into a priority list of work items. The group was now re-formed into four new work groups and each group was given a problem to manage. These new groups were carefully formed to make sure that a cross-section of people from all departments was included in each unit. Each group was asked to take the problem assigned and come up with answers to the following questions.

- What specific actions should be taken to deal with the problem area?
- Who should be responsible for the actions? (Give specific names.)
- Who should be responsible for supervising or managing the actions?
- When should the actions start and end?
- What should be the date for the first report of results?
- What rewards or penalties should be expected for success or failure to take action?

The groups worked hard at their tasks and late in the day they all came together to get the first group report. There was a serious discussion about the proposals made. People had to agree to assignments, deadlines, and the rewards and penalties. The consultant (who had been a roving observer and facilitator to the small groups) actively helped the group to look at the way it arrived at its final decisions. In addition, some problems in factions blocking each other, reactions to Chamberlain, and low commitment had to be worked out. But the group plugged away at the task until a final set of actions, to which all agreed, had been developed for every problem area.

By Friday afternoon, the staff was tired, but very satisfied. They had a complete list of action assignments with deadlines and dates for reporting progress. More important, they had experienced the satisfaction of honestly facing their real problems for the first time and felt successful in being able to work together in arriving at solutions that made sense to them. Many commented that this was the best work session they had ever had, and there was a sense of confidence that they could handle future problems more easily.

7

Follow-up
What Happens after the Team-Building Session

Remember: Team building is a process — not an event. Too many team-building programs have failed, not because the initial sessions were ineffective, but due to the lack of clear follow-up to ensure that the gains, agreements, and assignments made had been moved ahead.

Assuming that a team-building program began with some block of time that resulted in some agreements to change or improve the way team members have been functioning, how does a good follow-up program proceed?

There must be some method of following up with team members on assignments or agreements, and then some form of continuing goal setting for improved performance. These follow-up activities can either be done by the whole team together, one-to-one with team members, or a combination of the two. Fortunately, some excellent research has been done that describes the kinds of follow-up processes that have proven to be successful.

Professor Wayne Boss[1] of the University of Colorado be-

---

[1]R. Wayne Boss, "Team Building and the Problem of Regression: The Personal Management Interview as an Intervention," *Journal of Applied Behavioral Science 19*, no. 1 (1983).

came interested in the "regression" effect following a team-building session. He observed, as have others, that during a two- or three-day intensive team-building activity people became very enthusiastic about making improvements, but within a few weeks, the spark had dwindled and people had regressed to old performance levels. Boss's question: "Is there a way to keep performance high following the team-building session and to prevent the regression phenomenon from occurring?" He began to experiment with a one-to-one follow-up meeting he called the Personal Management Interview (PMI). The PMI had two stages — first, a role negotiation meeting between boss and subordinate (usually one hour) where both clarified their expectations of each other, what they needed from each other, and what they would eventually contract to do for each other.

Following the initial role negotiation session there were the regular PMIs between the two parties. Boss found that these meetings had to be held on a regular basis (weekly, biweekly, or monthly), but if they were held and followed the agreed-on agenda that performance stayed up without regression for periods up to three years. States Boss, "Without exception, the off-site levels of group effectiveness was maintained only in those teams that employed the PMI, while the teams that did not use the PMI evidenced substantial regression in the months after their team-building sessions."

What goes on in these interviews that makes such a difference? While there was some variation, each interview tended to deal with the following issues:

- Discussion of any organizational or work problems facing the subordinate
- Supervisor helping give training or coaching to subordinate
- Resolution of any concerns or problems between supervisor and subordinate
- Sharing of any information to bring subordinate up to date on what is happening in the organization
- Discussion of any personal problems or concerns

These were common agenda items, but the first part of every meeting was spent in reviewing assignments and accomplishments since the last session. Time was also spent in making new assignments and agreeing on goals and plans to be reviewed at the next PMI. These assignments and agreements were written down and each had a copy that was the basis of the review at the following meeting.

Boss has the following suggestions for conducting an effective PMI:

- The PMI is most effective when conducted in a climate of high support and trust. This is primarily the responsibility of the superior.
- The interviews must be held on a regular basis and be free from interruptions.
- Both parties must prepare for the meeting by having an agreed-on agenda; otherwise the PMI becomes nothing more than a "rap" session.
- When possible, a third party whom both supervisor and subordinate trust is present to take notes and record action items.
- Meetings are documented by use of a standard form on two-part carbonless paper. Both parties agree on the form.
- The leader must be willing to hold subordinates accountable and to ask the difficult "why" questions when assignments are not completed.

Boss has found that performance drops off if these meetings are not held but will increase if meetings are started, even if they had never been held before or had been stopped for a time. Certainly the evidence is compelling enough to indicate that this is an effective follow-up procedure.

The research by Boss does not talk about any further team sessions. Some units that have used the PMI have also reported having regular staff meetings to deal with issues common to all, and additional team development sessions, one every three to six months. These last mentioned sessions identify any current problems or concerns, and establish new change goals and plans for improvement.

In the past, many teams have followed up a team-building session with additional team meetings to review progress. The advantage of the PMI is that it allows more time to talk with each person on an individual basis. If this were done in the presence of the whole team it could be both inhibiting and extremely time-consuming.

Follow-up Team Sessions

In a good piece of research with sales teams, Rensis Likert[2] has described the elements of follow-up team meetings that make a significant difference in the performance of team members — in this case, sales personnel.

The research was done with sales offices from a national sales organization. The top twenty sales units were compared with the bottom twenty to see what made the difference. Likert found the following to be the most important factors:

- The sales manager who was the team leader had high personal performance goals and a plan for achieving these goals. Team members saw an example of high performance as they watched the team leader.
- The team leader personally displayed highly supportive behavior toward team members and encouraged team members to support each other.
- The team leader used participative methods in supervision. That is, all team members were involved in helping the team and the members achieve their goals.

The major process for achieving high performance was holding regular, well-planned meetings of the sales team for review of each person's performance. In contrast to Boss's PMI, which is a one-to-one follow-up, the units in the Likert research used team meetings as the follow-up process. Following are the major features of those team meetings:

- The team met regularly, every two weeks or every month.
- The size of the team would vary but was usually between twelve and fifteen members.
- The sales manager presided over the meeting but allowed wide participation in the group. The main function of the

---

[2]R. Likert, *The Human Organization* (New York: McGraw-Hill, 1967), Chap. 4.

manager was to keep the group focused on the task, push
the group to set high performance goals, and discourage
negative, nonsupportive, ego-deflating actions of team
members.

- Each sales person presented a report of his or her activities of the previous period including a description of approach used, closings attempted, and sales achieved, and
volume and quality of total sales.
- All the other team members then analyzed the person's
efforts and offered suggestions for improvement. Coaching was given by team members to each other.
- Each sales person would then announce his or her goals
and procedures to be used for review at the next team
meeting.

The researchers concluded that this form of team meeting
resulted in four benefits:

1. Sales people set higher goals.
2. They were more motivated to achieve their goals.
3. They received more assistance, coaching, and help from
boss and peers.
4. The group got more new ideas how to improve performance as people shared, not hid, their successful new
methods.

Likert summarizes these team meetings this way:

These group meetings are effective when the manager (or
supervisor) does a competent job of presiding over the interactions of the sales people. Appreciably poorer results
are achieved whenever the manager himself analyzes each
person's performance and results and sets goals for him.
Such man-to-man interactions in the meetings, dominated
by the manager, do not create group loyalty and have a far
less favorable impact on the salesman's motivation than
do group interactions and decision meetings. (p. 57)

It seems possible then to have either one-to-one follow-up
meetings or a series of follow-up team meetings as a way of maintaining high performance of team members. The key issue is that

team building means a continuous effort to monitor the team's ability to implement actions designed to improve team performance. The key person is the team leader, who must build in some type of follow-up procedure. Described in this chapter are two follow-up methods — one-to-one interviews and follow-up team meetings. There are other follow-up procedures available depending on the nature of the team's problems and plans.

It is possible to engage in a follow-up data-gathering process using some type of survey or questionnaire to see if unit members feel the activities of the team have improved. Another approach is to have an outsider come in and interview members to check on what has improved and what actions are still needed.

If the problem of the team is poor interaction at meetings, it is possible to follow up with the use of a procedure to get reactions of people after each meeting or after some meetings. The team leaders could use either a type of quick written form or ask for a critique of the meeting verbally, using the following questions: How satisfied were you with the team meeting today? Are there any actions we keep doing that restrict our effectiveness? What do we need to stop doing, start doing, or continue doing that would improve our team performance? Do we really function as a team or are there indications that teamwork is lacking? Are we achieving our goals and using each person's resources effectively?

If these questions are discussed, sufficient time needs to be allotted to do an adequate critique. If a written form is used, it could be filled out, summarized, and the next team meeting could begin with a review of the summary and a discussion of what should be done in the current meeting to make the team more effective.

It may also be possible to invite an outside observer to watch the team in action and give a process review at the end of the meeting.

Part III of this book describes several team-building designs. As a follow-up procedure, the team could implement one of these designs every six months or once a year as a way of seeing that improvements have been sustained.

Part III
Applications of Team Development

8

Developing the New Team

Team building is not just for existing units; it also can help a completely new unit mold a group of "strangers" into a workable team. New teams may either be temporary or of a more permanent nature. Most organizations at one time or another use various types of ad hoc groups, formed for a specific task and often for a limited duration. These are variously called task forces, committees, work groups, or project groups. When a new department is formed or units merge, a new working group that will function over a long period of time is created. In either case, the problem facing the unit is: How can we establish the kind of foundation, procedures, and programs that will maximize the possibility that we will be able to work together successfully?

The major tasks facing the new team are basically the same as for one that has worked together. They must build a relationship, establish a facilitative emotional climate, and work out methods for (1) setting goals, (2) solving problems, (3) making decisions, (4) ensuring follow-through and completion of tasks, (5) developing collaboration of effort, (6) establishing lines of open communication, and (7) ensuring an appropriate support system that will let people feel accepted and yet keep issues open for discussion and disagreement. The advantage the new team has over an old established unit in a team-building situation is that it does not have to break down any barriers, bad habits, useless or harmful stereotypes or attitudes, inappropriate working relations, or procedures that have been formed and are sometimes set rigidly in the concrete of human habit. In a new unit where members have had some previous working relationships, there may be some residues of ineffective feelings or actions that may need to be handled. Generally the new team can start its activities by asking: How can we set in motion the kinds of actions that will allow us to work together and get our goals accomplished and leave us feeling good about ourselves and each other?

The Effective Committee

If we take a newly formed committee as an example of a unit interested in new team development, there is evidence that people enter into this new assignment with certain positive and negative expectations. One survey of nearly 200 university-based people with committee or task-force assignments came up with the following data.

Reasons Why People Do Not Like to Serve on a Committee or Task Force

1. Poor leadership. The leader fails to keep the discussion on the subject, to monitor and direct to keep things moving in the appropriate direction, and to engage in those activities that are stimulating and motivating to the members.
2. Goals are unclear. Members are not really sure what they are trying to accomplish.
3. Assignments are not taken seriously by committee members. There is an apparent lack of commitment.
4. There is a lack of focus on the committee's assignment ("What are we supposed to be doing today?").
5. Recommendations of the committee are often ignored by top management. Management needs to be more responsive to the committee.

6. Waste of time. Unproductive discussions of problems, with no conclusions or decisions made.
7. Lack of follow-through with assignments on the part of committee members.
8. Often a domination by one person or clique. Some talk and push for their positions, while others wonder why they are there.
9. Lack of preparation by committee members, including the chairman of the meeting. Agenda not prepared, materials and things that really need to be there are not available. Someone has not done his homework.
10. No action taken. The committee spends a lot of time without coming up with specific items resulting in some kind of action.
11. People often have hidden agendas, personal axes to grind. They get into discussions that only one or two think are important.

Things People Like about Committees or a Task Force When They Function Well

1. Clear role definition of the committee — what the committee and its members are supposed to do, what their goals are.
2. Careful time control. Starting on time and ending on time. Enough time allowed to get the work done and no more.
3. Committee members are sensitive to each other's needs and expressions. People listen to and respect others' opinions.
4. There is an informal relaxed atmosphere, rather than a formal exchange.
5. Good preparation on the part of the chairman and committee members. Materials prepared and available.
6. Members all qualified and interested. They want to be a part of the committee. A definite commitment exists.
7. Interruptions are avoided or held to a minimum.
8. Good minutes or records are kept, so that decisions are

not lost. There is no need to search out what decisions were made.

9. Periodically, the committee stops and assesses its own performance. Needed improvements are worked out.
10. Committee members feel they are given some kind of reward for their committee efforts. Recognition and appreciation are given, so that they feel they are really making a contribution.
11. The work of the committee is accepted and used, and seems to make a contribution to the organization.

This survey suggests that it would be wise for the newly formed committee to spend enough time initially planning how it will work to avoid those activities that bother people and how it will incorporate those to which people respond. All of the recent work on quality circles indicates that many of the same issues that bog down a committee or task force also hinder the quality circle groups.

Design for a New Committee Team

In this team-building session, members meet long enough for people to get acquainted and to set guidelines and procedures for work.

Step 1. Developing a Realistic Priority Level

It often occurs that people who are put together on a new team, frequently by assignment, have widely differing levels of priority or commitment to the work assigned. Some may see it as a highly significant assignment and worthy of a great deal of time and energy. Others may see it as important, but lower on their personal priority list, while still others may see it as low in both importance and priority. One method for coming to grips with the priority issue is the following.

a. Have each person draw a vertical line that represents his or her total work requirements and the priorities for them. Each person puts a mark at the point that represents where this team assignment ranks as a priority activity. See Figure 8–1.

Figure 8–1
Priority and Time Rankings

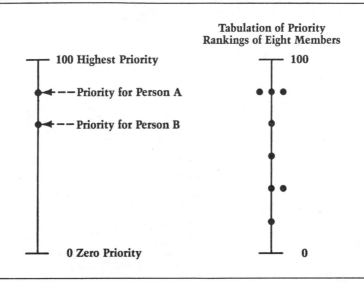

b. Next, have each person write down the amount of time he or she would be willing to commit to the work of the team over a month's time.

c. Summarize the priority rankings (see Fig. 8–1) and also the time commitments. See the range of times and priorities and also the averages for the two dimensions.

d. In the group, let each person who desires explain his or her priority and time rankings and then come to agreement as to a realistic amount of time and energy that can be expected of the team as a whole. Persons with higher priority and team commitments may be allowed to accept heavier assignments. Making this decision openly reduces the resentment some have for doing more work and the guilt of others for letting them.

Understanding the priority of time and commitment is especially important for a temporary team. This step may not be useful for a new team that will continue to stay together.

Step 2. Sharing Expectations

Give five minutes for each person to think about and get ready to respond to the following questions:

    a. What worries you most or is your biggest concern about working on this team?
    b. How would this team function if everything went just as you would hope?
    c. What would this team be like if everything went wrong?
    d. What actions do you think must be taken to ensure the positive outcomes?

Each person has an opportunity to share reactions; everyone responds to each question in turn. Try to identify the major concerns people have and list them on a blackboard or newsprint. These concerns should become items on a planning agenda as conditions to take into consideration in order to ensure that positive things are achieved.

Step 3. Clarifying Goals

At this point, having now established the priority and commitment level and identified positive and negative expectations, the new team is ready to clarify its goals and objectives. The team should discuss and then write down what members agree is the *core mission* of the group. This is a statement of the basic function or "reason for being" for that group, committee, or team. All plans and actions should be evaluated against the core mission. The question to constantly ask is: If we continue the activities already outlined, will we accomplish our core mission? Extending from the core mission are the subgoals and specific objectives for a given period of time.

For example, the Edgemont Company formed a task force to review all training and development activities in the company and to come up with some recommendations for a coordinated training and development effort. The task force met and established its core mission: The mission of this task force is to ensure an appropriate and effective thrust in management and organization development in the Edgemont Company.

Subgoals were then identified. The team agreed to try to

accomplish the core mission by (a) reviewing all ongoing training and development programs; (b) assessing the effectiveness of these programs; (c) determining if there are any overlaps or major gaps in training and development; (d) constructing a model of an effective program; (e) making recommendations to the executive committee as to the type of program needed; (f) assisting, if needed, in the implementation of the recommendations; and (g) assisting in evaluating the consequences or results of the implemented recommendations.

Having set the core mission and specific subgoals, the task force is now ready to make specific assignments to task-force members.

Step 4. Formulating Operating Guidelines

The new team needs to establish guidelines for how it will work during the course of its existence. Provisions also need to be formulated for changing the guidelines if they prove to be dysfunctional or inappropriate as conditions change. Following are some of the areas for which guidelines may be useful. The guidelines should clarify actions and roles and should reduce the ambiguity or mixed expectations of people as to how things ought to function, which is the basis of a great deal of conflict in a working group.

How Will We Make Decisions? It is useful for the new team to talk about its decision-making procedures. Do they want to make decisions by majority vote, team consensus, or leave some decisions to subgroups that are assigned to work?

If the group opts to make decisions by consensus, all should realize that this does not mean unanimity (everyone thinking alike). A consensus is a decision hammered out by permitting everyone to have a say. After discussion and give-and-take and compromise has occurred, consensus is reached when people honestly can say, "This is a sound decision — one that I am willing *to support and implement.* It is not exactly what I personally want, but given the range of opinions, the time factor, and the kinds of personalities involved, it is a good, working decision."

Unless *everyone* can take the position described above, a

consensus has not been reached. Discussion would need to continue and adjustments or compromises or new alternatives would have to be explored until a solution is found that results in team consensus.

What Will Be Our Basic Method for Work? The team should decide what it feels will be the most efficient way to get work done. Should they have all items considered by the total group, have people do individual work that is then submitted to the group, or have subcommittees do the initial work? It is possible that all of the above may be used, depending on the nature of the work to be done. However, the method of work should be decided at the outset.

How Do We Make Sure Everyone Gets a Chance to Discuss Issues or Raise Concerns? If a team is to be effective, members need to feel that they are able to discuss and have considered issues or concerns they deem important. How will the team ensure this condition? It may be agreed that any member can put any item of concern on the agenda for the next meeting. There may be an "open" meeting scheduled periodically to allow discussion of any topic or issue. Time could be reserved at the end of certain meetings for an open discussion. Members could be asked to distribute a memo identifying the issue they want discussed.

How Will We Resolve Differences? In any working group there will be times when individuals or subgroups disagree. If not handled or managed, disagreements can, at the least, waste time, and may even split the group into warring factions. A guideline for dealing with differences can be useful. If two people or subgroups disagree, it may be more useful to have a guideline that recommends they get together (sometimes with a mediator) outside of the meeting of the whole group to work out their differences rather than holding up the actions of the entire team. A third person or subunit could be appointed to listen to both sides of the issues and then recommend possible compromises or new alternatives. Time limits for the open discussion of differences might expedite reaching a conclusion (or might be a frustrating hindrance). A majority voting procedure might be appropriate if the group can honestly adopt a "loyal opposition" position that allows people the right to disagree or vote differently but still implement actions.

Whatever the method for discussion, understanding, and resolving issues, a guideline will provide a beginning for coping with the sensitive problem of differences that may occur.

How Will We Ensure the Completion of Work? One of the major problems in working in groups (particularly of the committee or task-force variety) is the frustrating experience of some people coming unprepared or failing to complete assignments. How can the team face that issue constructively? The guidelines may suggest that no one will be given or will accept an assignment if the person honestly knows he or she will not invest an appropriate amount of energy in its preparation. This means there must be a realistic level of priority building (see step 1) and a trusting enough climate that people will feel free to state their honest preferences and reactions to assignments. This guideline may outline a procedure for having the chairman or other designated leader remind every person with an assignment at a suitable time prior to the next meeting. An action summary of every meeting will clearly identify all assignments and dates for report and completion, as illustrated in the following sample.

Action Summary (Sample)

Decision	Who Is to Do What	Date for Completion	Date to Report Progress
1. It was agreed there would be a training seminar for all supervisors on June 15.	1. John Hicks will make all physical arrangements.	June 10	Next meeting— May 20
	2. Ann Stewart will contact the three possible resource people.	May 24	Next meeting— May 20

The action summary can be used in place of minutes or in addition to regular narrative minutes, but it should clearly pinpoint assignments and times for completion. If a person fails to complete an assignment, the guideline may suggest an appropriate action, such as a personal visit by the chairman, a report and explanation to the committee, or some other review mechanism.

How Will We Change Things That Are Not Producing Results? There should be some guidelines for reviewing the way the committee or team has been working and a method for making changes when guidelines or procedures or even people in certain positions are no longer achieving results. This guideline may suggest a periodic evaluation session when the team honestly looks at its own work, reviews its successes and failures, and asks the question, "What changes would make the team more effective?" If guideline 3 has been operating effectively, many issues will have been covered, but the team may need to agree on a periodic review and evaluation meeting, or that any person could call for such a meeting when he or she felt conditions warranted it.

Again, the success of such a meeting depends on people feeling free to express their honest views about the team's effectiveness and to make recommendations for improvement. A fearful, defensive group will find it hard to plan useful changes.

New Teams in Action

What are the differences between a work group that plans for its own successful functioning and one that plunges into work and hopes everything turns out all right? Consider the following two cases.

The Deans' Council, State University

With the arrival of a new president, a number of positions at the deans' level were changed; new people moved into some positions and reassignments were made for others. When the new academic vice-president met with all of the current deans, his desire was to get the group involved quickly in the matters of concern to the new administration. He spent the first twenty minutes allowing each dean the opportunity to introduce himself or herself and to take two minutes to say something about his or her particular college. As usual, some talked beyond their two minutes, but most kept to the stated limit.

The vice-president then outlined the major tasks of the council as he saw them, asked for everyone's cooperation, and set the time for the next meeting. Much to his dismay, the vice-president discovered that the council did not move ahead as he expected. At nearly every meeting, 30 to 40 percent of the deans were absent and an associate dean was there representing the chief. The functioning of the council was erratic. Sometimes a few people dominated the discussion and the others sat silent; at other times, people seemed divided into two camps and decisions were polarized between these two factions. The vice-president was reluctant to make final decisions that were opposed by such a large number of powerful deans, so he tabled many of the decisions while "further aspects of the problem were investigated." Clearly this group was going to be a tough one to manage.

The Deans' Council, Union University

When the new deans' council was formed, Martha Allen, the recently appointed academic vice-president, spent a lot of time thinking about how to get that group of highly skilled, variously trained people to work together for common university goals. She asked each dean to clear one full day to meet at a retreat center for planning the way the council would work during the coming year.

At the first meeting in the morning, Allen described what she felt were the major functions of the deans' council and what she hoped they might accomplish. She then asked each dean to stand, introduce himself or herself if new to the group, and share his or her views about the council in regard to two questions: (1) What would the council be like if everything functioned ideally? and (2) What would the council be like if everything went wrong and it was a total disaster? Allen began the process by frankly describing her hopes and fears for the council. Each dean then followed and the comments were very frank and insightful.

Allen then asked the deans to divide into small groups. There were eighteen present, so they divided into three groups of six people. Each group was asked to consider the question: What will we need to do (how shall we organize and how shall we function) to ensure that the workings of this council are successful?

After an hour's discussion, the three groups reported back the results of their discussion. Each group listed its recommendations as to the actions needed to ensure success. These included such things as the need for regular meeting times when all can be in attendance, defined agendas announced in advance, subcommittees to deal with continuing problems, regular meetings with the president, an administrative assistant in the vice-president's office to follow up on action items, and clear communications as to changes and developments from the president's office. Almost all of the recommendations were agreed on and action decisions made on those for which a decision was appropriate.

The vice-president then asked the small groups each to take one problem and come up with recommendations. Group 1 was asked to consider: How shall we make decisions in the council? Should all decisions be by majority vote, by consensus, or sometimes one or the other? Group 2 discussed: How shall the council function to ensure open discussion of all issues without getting bogged down in lengthy, unproductive discussion? Group 3 had the assignment: How shall we critique the council's activities to see if we are achieving our goals, and how shall we determine if someone is not satisfied with the way the council is working?

After intense discussion, the groups presented their recommendations to the council and a set of operating guidelines were adopted. People left the workshop with a sense of satisfaction about the accomplishments of the day, optimism about the coming year, and a greater feeling of integration with each other and the administration.

New teams do not have to wait until problems arise and the negative consequences force some type of remedial action. A team can plan for its future and build in procedures for continually assessing its own functioning. Given this feedback, it can regularly take actions to ensure the team stays on target with its goals. Such planning is the major goal of a development program for the new team or work unit.

9

Conflict Problems
in the Ongoing Team

The team that has been together for some time often has
a different set of problems or concerns from the new team. The
diagnosis may identify conditions of frustration, antagonism,
misunderstandings, hurt feelings, and conflict. When the diagnosis identifies these kinds of issues, a different team-building
format is needed.

Sometimes a group has worked together for years, but
either basic assignments were never clarified or conditions have
changed and old role definitions are no longer adequate. Following is a description of a team-building model designed to reduce
problems arising out of unclear assignments or relationships.
Most teams have never spent adequate time making sure all
members understand their roles and what is expected of them.

The Role-Clarification Model

The role-clarification model of team building is considered
appropriate if several of the following conditions are prevalent in
the organization or unit considering a team-building program.[1]

[1]See I. Dayol and J. M. Thomas, "Operation KPE: Developing a New
Organization," *The Journal of Applied Behavioral Science 4*, no. 4 (1968):473–506,
for a discussion of the RAT Technique, similar to this discussion.

1. The unit is newly organized and people are not clear as to what others do and what others expect of them.
2. Changes and reassignments have been made in the unit and there is a lack of clarity as to how the various functions and positions now fit together under the new arrangements.
3. Original job descriptions are old. Staff meetings are held infrequently and then only for passing on needed directions. People carry out their assignments with very little contact with others in the same office. People generally feel isolated.
4. Conflicts and disruptions between people in the unit seem to be increasing. Coffee-break talk and other information communications center around discussions of overlaps and encroachments on work assignments from others. People get requests they don't understand. People hear about what others are doing via the grapevine and it sounds like something they should know about but nobody gets them together.
5. The boss engages primarily in one-to-one management. Staff meetings are infrequent or are primarily held for hearing the boss raise issues with one individual at a time while others watch and wait for their turn. Almost no problem solving is done as a total staff or between people. Issues are taken to the boss and only then are needed people called together.
6. People sit in their offices and wonder, "What is happening in this outfit? I don't know what others are doing and I'm sure nobody knows (or cares) what I'm doing."
7. A crisis occurs because everyone thought someone else was responsible for handling a situation that was never covered.

Planning

Time Commitment. Assuming a staff of eight to ten people, the minimum time needed for this type of design is approximately one hour for each person or a total of eight to ten hours of meeting time, preferably a solid block of time. Assuming a training day from 8:30 to 12:00 and 1:00 to 4:30, this could be achieved in one and a half training days. It would also be possible to conduct this type of team-building session by taking out one afternoon a week over a period of time, such as three afternoons in one week, or one afternoon for three weeks. Our experience indicates that the time spent in one block allows for more impact to occur. Each time a group meets, a certain amount of "settling-in" time occurs, which is minimized if the sessions are held at one time.

Resource Personnel. If the ground rules, procedures, overall goals, and design elements are clear, this format is one where a manager need not be afraid to conduct this type of meeting with no outside assistance from a consultant or facilitator. If certain realistic concerns suggest that an outside person would be helpful in facilitating the meeting, this type of resource person could be included. This person may be someone from within the company, but in a different department (such as an OD specialist), or a consultant from outside the company entirely.

Whether or not an outside resource person is used, the whole team-building meeting should be conducted and "managed" by the senior administrator or boss. Team building is management's business; it is a supervisor building his or her team. It is *not* an exercise called by a staff person in personnel.

Program Design

Goal. The goal of a role relationship team-building program is to arrive at that condition in the work unit where all unit members can publicly agree that they

> have a clear understanding of the major requirements of their own job;
>
> feel that the others at the team-building meeting also clearly understand everyone's position and duties;
>
> know what others expect of them in their working relationships;
>
> feel that all know what others need from them in their working relationships.

All agreements in working relationships are met in a spirit of collaboration and a willingness to implement the understandings. Procedures are established that permit future misunderstandings to be handled in a more effective way.

Preparation. This part of the team-building activity can be done prior to coming to the session, or should be done first by each member of the group in private as the team session begins. Each person should prepare answers to the following questions:

1. What do you feel the organization expects you to do in your job? (This may include the formal job description.)
2. What do you actually do in your job? (Describe your actual working activities and point out any discrepancies between the formal job description and your actual job activities.)
3. Identify specific difficulties or concerns you have had in working with other team members.
4. What do you need to know about other people's jobs that would help you do your work?
5. What do you feel others should know about your job that would help them do their work?
6. What do you need from others in order to do your job the way you would like?

Meeting Design

All meetings of the team-building program should be conducted by the unit manager. If a consultant is present, he or she should be a resource, but should not conduct the sessions.

Goals. The goals of the team-building meeting should be presented and clarified and discussed. Everyone should agree on the goals or hoped-for outcomes of the sessions.

Ground Rules. Ground rules for functioning should be developed from the group, written on a sheet of paper, and posted for all to see. Some suggested ground rules follow:

1. Each person should be as candid and open as possible in a spirit of wanting to help improve the team.
2. If a person wants to know how another person feels or what that person thinks on an issue, he or she should ask that person directly. The person asked should give an honest response, even if it is to say, "I don't feel like responding right now."
3. If the meeting becomes unproductive for any person, he or she should express this concern to the group.
4. Each person should have an opportunity to speak on every issue.
5. Decisions made should be agreeable to all persons affected by the decision.

Job Understanding. Each person will be the focal person and should have a chance to read his or her answers to preparatory questions 1, 2, and 5 describing what he or she feels he or she should be doing in his or her assignment or role. After the focal person reads an answer, all other team members should have a chance to respond in terms of how they have seen that person's job and what they feel he or she should be doing. It is important for each person to hear how others see his or her job, and also what they would like the person to do on the job that would be of benefit to them. Each person should be given ample time to explore personal job responsibilities with others. This could be from thirty minutes to more than an hour for each person.

Each person should next read his or her answers to question 4 and attempt to get answers from the person(s) identified in the question in the total group. An alternative design is to have group members read their answers to question 4 and then arrange for individual interviews so that people can talk with the individuals they mentioned in their responses.

Concerns. Each person should read his or her answer to question 3. Many of these concerns may have already been covered in the earlier discussions, but any unresolved concerns should be aired at this time.

As much as possible, try to solve problems and not place blame. It is not as important to fix blame on a person as it is to recognize that a problem exists and to work out a solution.

Need for Others. Each person should read his or her answer to question 6. It is important that people talk with each other as to what they need from each other in order for them to be effective. The focal person tells others what is needed from them and the others also explain what they need from the focal person.

Conclusion. At the end of the sessions, the whole team-building program should be critiqued. People should respond to the following questions:

1. How have you felt about the team-building meetings?
2. What were the best parts for you?
3. What needed to be changed or improved?
4. Do we need other sessions like this? If so, what should we discuss? When should we meet again?

This type of team-development meeting is one of the easiest to manage and one of the most productive of all design possibilities for improving team effectiveness. Most groups of people slip into areas of ambiguity in their working relationships. Expectations get formed about performances which people do not understand or even know about. The periodic clarification of roles is a useful process for any working group.

One company's executive committee was conducting a role-clarification meeting. The members of the president's management group were outlining their jobs as they saw them, and what they felt they needed from each other in order to carry out their jobs more effectively. When it came to the personnel manager, she turned to the president and said, "One of the actions I need from you is a chance to get together with you a couple of times a year and review my performance and see what things you feel I need to do to improve."

The president asked in surprise, "Why do you need to get together with me?"

Responded the personnel manager, "When I was hired two years ago, it was my understanding that I was to report directly to you."

"Nobody ever cleared that with me," stated the president. "I thought you reported to the executive vice-president."

The personnel manager had been waiting for two years for

a chance to get directions and instructions from the person she thought was her direct superior, but that relationship had never been clarified until the role-clarification session. It's almost like having the center on a football team not know that he is supposed to hike the ball to the quarterback.

The Team in Conflict

At times it can be observed that the basic problem in a work unit is the prevalence of highly disruptive conflict and hostility. In some departments, feelings of animosity between individuals or between cliques or subgroups have grown to such proportions that people who must work together do not speak to each other at all. Communications are all by memo, even though offices are adjoining. Why do such conflicts occur and how can a work group resolve such differences? Probably the most common "explanation" for understanding conflict is the theory of conflicting personalities. When two people do not get along, a commonplace explanation is to say their "personalities" clash. Underlying this is a presumption that the personality of one (a complex of attitudes, values, feelings, needs, and experiences) is so different from the personality of the other that they just cannot function compatibly. Since one's personality is so deeply rooted by the adult stage of life, it seems almost impossible to improve the situation.

Expectation Theory of Conflict

A more useful way to understand conflict is to view it as the result of a violation of expectations. Whenever the behavior of one person violates the expectations of another, it can be predicted that negative reactions will result. If agreements are not reached, the continued cycle of violated expectations and the application of negative sanctions can escalate until open expressions of hostility are common and people are trying to hurt or punish the other in various ways rather than trying to work cooperatively. It should be noted that people have expectations of others in terms of *what* is to be done, *when* it should be done, and *how* it is to be done. Frequently people may agree on the "what" conditions but the violations occur in when actions should be taken, or how they should be fulfilled.

One R&D department in a large corporation was split by conflict. There were two warring factions of professionals. For some reason, one group of development researchers felt that the other group got more favors, better facilities, and more rewards than they did. Their expectations were continually being violated. They expected more sharing of research results, more common decision making, more meetings, more equal distribution of rewards. When these expectations were not met, they reacted negatively. These negative responses in turn violated the expectations of the other faction and they reciprocated with their own critical reactions. Before long, the department was filled with unpleasant feelings of hostility.

Expectation theory allows for a greater possibility for dealing with conflict, for it focuses on behavior. If the one faction in the R&D department can begin to identify the behaviors or actions that violate their expectations, perhaps agreements can be negotiated, so that the end result is people rewarding each other rather than applying punishments.

Negotiating Agreements

In planning a team-building session to deal with conflicts, certain agreements between the clashing parties need to be met: (1) All parties must agree to come together and work on the problems. (2) It helps if people can agree that there are problems, that these problems should be solved, and that all parties have some responsibility to work on the issues. (3) People may find it easier to deal with conflict if they can accept the position that the end result of the team-building session is not to get everyone to "like" one another, but to understand one another and to be able to work together. It is not necessary that everyone form personal friendships, but group members should be able to at least trust each other and meet one another's expectations.

In setting up the team-building session, the disagreeing parties will work best together if they can adopt the position that it is not productive to try and unravel who is at fault or what "caused" the problems; rather, they should accept the fact that differences exist and they need to work out agreeable solutions.

The Start-Stop-Continue Format

When the parties come together in the team-building session, each party builds a list for the other. Each lists the things they would like to see the other individual or group start doing, stop doing, and continue to do if their expectations are to be met and positive results achieved. The parties then share their lists with each other. If there is general conflict in the team — not between parties — each person lists what the total team needs to start doing, stop doing, or continue to do to reduce conflicts and disruptions.

Negotiation

With the lists of things that each party wants from the other on display for all to see, a negotiation session ensues. Subgroup or person A identifies what it wants from subgroup or person B and vice versa. The two units then agree on what one party will do in return for an equal behavioral alteration on the part of the other. Such agreements can actually be written up. In some cases, signing the agreement increases the commitment to making the change. Such a process puts the formerly warring factions into a problem-solving situation that requires them to try to work out solutions rather than spending their time finding fault, placing blame, or looking for causes of the problems. This negotiation process has been described by Harrison[2] and has been the basis for a companywide team-development program in the Diamond Shamrock Company.[3]

The design of such a conflict-reducing meeting can vary widely. It may be desirable to precede the session with a presentation of expectation theory and to describe the negative consequences of continued hostility. Another possibility is to have members of each party try to predict what the other party thinks

---

[2]R. Harrison, "Role Negotiations," in W. Burke and H. Hornstein, *The Social Technology of Organization Development* (Washington, D.C.: NTL Learning Resources, 1971).

[3]Arthur M. Louis, "They're Striking Some Strange Bargains at Diamond Shamrock," *Fortune*, January 1976, pp. 142–157.

about them and what they think the other wants from them. These guesses are often surprisingly accurate and may facilitate the coming to agreement.

This design may also be used to negotiate agreements between individuals. If a manager feels the thing most divisive in the team is conflict between two people, the manager can bring these people together and get them into a problem-solving situation where they begin to work out agreements with one another. If there are disagreements in the team at any point, it is often well to stop and work out a negotiation and come to an agreement. Negotiation is often a compromise situation. Each party gives up something to receive something of similar value from the other. Too frequently conflicts are handled by people engaging in the following behaviors:

1. Ignoring. This means trying to pretend there is no real disagreement at all.
2. Smoothing. Here the attempt is to try to placate people and attempt to get people to feel good even though an agreement has not been reached.
3. Forcing. When one party has more power than the other, the powerful person may try to force the other to agree. This may result in public agreement but private resistance.

In an effective team, when conflict occurs, time is taken to identify the cause of the conflict; it is identified as a problem to be solved and problem-solving actions are taken.

10

Revitalizing the Complacent Team

Problems on a New Job

When Scott Roberts, a new MBA, accepted a position in a medium-sized foods company, he was excited about the prospects of his first major job. He hoped to put to use all of his training and he had some ideas that he felt were good which he wanted to share with others in the organization. In didn't take Scott long to learn that people didn't seem to want his bright ideas. After nine months, Scott was convinced that the only people who got ahead in the organization were those who kept their mouths shut, did what they were told, and constantly affirmed their loyalty to the company. Staff meetings were always very pleasant. People went along with whatever the person in charge recommended. Every meeting was conducted the same way; even the agenda items were almost always the same.

People seemed to like their jobs and the company. Most of the personnel had been with the company for more than fifteen years and seemed to be satisfied to continue in the same pattern until retirement. Scott's attempts to raise questions and put in some new suggestions were met with an indulgent smile from his boss, who told him that they "liked the 'fire' in the new people, to keep the ideas coming, and they would take his suggestions under advisement." Scott heard no more about them.

When Scott expressed concerns about his job to his wife, she wanted to know what was wrong with the company. Scott had a hard time putting his finger on anything concrete. People treated him well, his work went smoothly, the future seemed secure. Everything was "just fine" and that was the rub. Scott knew he wanted more out of his work. He needed more challenge, greater stimulation, more exchange, and a chance to match wits with other people. Scott could not help feeling that this company could not hold its own over the long haul against competitors who were aggressively looking at the conditions of the market and coming up with new products that were capturing the attention of the buying public. Scott began seriously to reevaluate his future and his fit with the current company.

A company like the one Scott belongs to could benefit from a program designed to look at its own complacency and lack of innovation and aggressive action concerning the present and future. Teams in this organization are like the baseball team that has become "fat and happy." They may win for a while longer, but the teams that are hungrier, with more desire, more energy, and more thrust, are going to emerge and begin to move ahead. There are many conditions that threaten the effectiveness of a working team, and the lack of imagination and creativity is an eroding spirit that can be met and managed with the right kind of action.

The original team-development designs were created primarily to help deal with issues centered mostly around matters of conflict, disruption, ineffective methods, unclear assignments or expectations, and leadership problems. These generally are areas where something needs to be repaired or a problem solved. However, some organizations or units find that the issue is not a matter of an unsolved problem or a case of disruption, but a situation where people have drifted into a common, routine, standard, accepted way of "doing business." If this kind of team were to be "developed" to improve its effectiveness, the thrust would be in the direction of stimulating greater creativity, more innovation in finding new products or services, more imaginative programs, and new ways to work, thus developing a more zestful, stimulating climate. It has also been shown that often a creative person is an individualist in thinking and acting. To build a team that fosters creativity may require a change of norms that allows more individual freedom and idiosyncratic behavior. At first this may seem antithetical to building a team with a goal of having everyone fit in and conform to the group norms. The creative team may need to become looser and less structured in order to become more creative.

Diagnosis

If the following conditions appear, it may be useful for the work unit to consider a team-development program with the goal of stimulating greater imagination and creativity.

- The same people seem to be doing the same things the same ways year after year, even though other conditions have changed.
- Products or service levels have stayed constant for some years, although similar factors in other organizations have improved.
- New people often transfer out or quit because the atmosphere is just not challenging enough.
- The area of greatest pride among workers is their devotion and loyalty to the organization.
- There seems to be a fear or resistance to risk-taking behavior or trying out something new.
- The rewards in the organization go to the people who do the solid, standard job. Few rewards go to the person who initiates a new method or product.

A work unit with several of these conditions might be one where people trust and respect each other and feel good about their manager, where conflicts and disruptions are minimal, and where serious employee or work problems seldom emerge. One might feel that such a unit would be "ideal" and would have no need for a development program. However, if it is seen that external conditions have changed, new demands are present, the old methods are not keeping pace, and young progressive people are choosing other organizations, then perhaps a revitalizing team-development program is appropriate.

Steiner[1] has identified the following as some of the characteristics of a creative organization.

1. The creative organization includes marginal, unusual types of people.
2. It has open channels of communication.
3. It encourages contacts with outside sources.
4. The organization experiments with new ideas rather than prejudging on "rational" grounds; everything gets a chance.
5. It is not run as a "tight ship."
6. Employees have fun.
7. Rewards go to people with ideas.
8. Ideas are evaluated on their merits, not according to the status of the originator.
9. New, ad hoc approaches are allowed to emerge.
10. There is a risk-taking ethos; the organization tolerates and expects taking chances.

The scale presented in Figure 10–1 may help you diagnose the level of creativity allowed on the job. At least two problems in creativity might be identified:

1. All people in the organization or unit may be generally satisfied with what an outside observer might assess as a routine, safe, uncreative climate.
2. Some members of the unit may desire greater support for innovation and change, but other parts of the system repress or deny this.

Before any team-development activity would occur, someone with influence would have to recognize the above conditions existing in the work unit as unproductive, and would have to move for some type of change. Recently much has been written

---

[1]Gary Steiner, *The Creative Organization* (Chicago: University of Chicago Press, 1965).

Figure 10-1
Encouraging Creativity Through Management and Organization[*]

This scale will help you see to what extent the type of management and the organizational conditions support and encourage creative effort.

1. My ideas or suggestions never get a fair hearing. 1 2 3 4 5 6 7 My ideas or suggestions always get a fair hearing.

2. I feel that my boss is not interested in my ideas. 1 2 3 4 5 6 7 I feel that my boss is very interested in my ideas.

3. I receive no encouragement to innovate on my job. 1 2 3 4 5 6 7 I am encouraged to innovate on my job.

4. There is no reward for innovating or improving things on my job. 1 2 3 4 5 6 7 I am rewarded for innovating and improving on my job.

5. There is no encouragement for diverse opinions among subordinates. 1 2 3 4 5 6 7 There is encouragement of diversity of opinion among subordinates.

6. I'm very reluctant to tell the boss about mistakes I make. 1 2 3 4 5 6 7 I feel comfortable enough with my boss to tell about mistakes I make.

7. I'm not given enough responsibility to do my job right. 1 2 3 4 5 6 7 I am given enough responsibility to do my job right.

(cont.)

Figure 10–1 (*cont.*)

8. To really succeed in this organization, one needs to be a friend or a relative of the boss.	1 2 3 4 5 6 7	There is no favoritism in the organization.
9. There are other jobs in this organization that I would prefer to have.	1 2 3 4 5 6 7	I have the job in this organization that I think I do best.
10. They keep close watch over me too much of the time.	1 2 3 4 5 6 7	They trust me to do my job without always checking on me.
11. They would not let me try other jobs in the organization.	1 2 3 4 5 6 7	I could try other kinds of jobs in the organization if I wanted to.
12. The management is made very uptight by confusion, disorder, and chaos.	1 2 3 4 5 6 7	The management deals easily with confusion, disorder, and chaos.
13. There is a low standard of excellence on the job.	1 2 3 4 5 6 7	There is a high standard of excellence on the job.

Figure 10–1 (cont.)

#	Statement	Scale	Statement
14.	My boss is not open to receive my opinion of how he/she might improve his/her own performance on the job.	1 2 3 4 5 6 7	My boss is very open to suggestions on how he/she might improve his/her own performance on the job.
15.	My boss has a very low standard for judging his/her own performance.	1 2 3 4 5 6 7	My boss has a very high standard for judging his/her own performance.
16.	I am not asked for suggestions on how to improve service to the customers.	1 2 3 4 5 6 7	The management actively solicits my suggestions and ideas on how to improve service to the customers.
17.	My boss shows no enthusiasm for the work we are engaged in.	1 2 3 4 5 6 7	My boss exhibits lots of enthusiasm for the work we are engaged in.
18.	Mistakes get you in trouble; they aren't to learn from.	1 2 3 4 5 6 7	Around here mistakes are to learn from and not to penalize you.
19.	Someone else dictates how much I should accomplish on my job.	1 2 3 4 5 6 7	I'm allowed to set my own goals for my job.
20.	The organization has too many rules and regulations for me.	1 2 3 4 5 6 7	The organization has adequate rules and regulations for me.

* By Philip B. Daniels and William G. Dyer.

about fostering creativity inside organizations, identifying the process of "intrepreneurship." Kanter[2] and others have noted that organizations need to provide a procedure for people with ideas to get connected with a person with power (a champion) who will help move an idea along. This suggests that innovation must be an organization's goal as well as a team objective.

Design Elements

Data Gathering

Since a team moving along in a "standard" manner may not feel a need for more innovation, there needs to be some process for showing unit members that the usual ways of doing things are not enough and that change, creativity, and innovation must be encouraged. This might be done in the following ways.

1. Gather comparative data showing the performance of this unit compared to other, more innovative, similar groups.
2. If the unit is a pocket of conservatism, gather comments from other units who are able to see the conditions more clearly, and present them so that unit members can see their image in the eyes of others.
3. Interview unit members to discover whether some are aware of the situation, even though they find it comfortable and satisfying.
4. Management may need to give unit members an honest appraisal of the conditions they see existing.

If the unit tends to discourage creativity to the distress of some members, such conditions can be surfaced by interviews, instruments such as found in Figure 10–1, a problem census, or the observations of a process consultant.

For this type of development program, an initial data-gathering phase to surface the need and the reasons for initiating the program is a necessary first step.

---

[2]R. Kanter, *The Change Masters* (New York: Simon and Schuster, 1983).

Data Sharing and Diagnosis

In this phase, unit members are presented with a summary of the data that have been collected. Group members are then asked to look at the data and discuss the reasons why such conditions exist and what could be changed, and to agree on some new goals for improvement.

Action Planning

In this phase, actions to be taken can be planned by the whole unit, subgroups with assignments, or a task force with the charge to review the creativity level of the unit and to come up with recommendations for change.

Since the area of creative action may be unfamiliar to the team members, they may need to be supplied with some possible actions that could be taken to stimulate innovation in their work unit, as follows:

- Conduct seminars on creative thinking.
- Establish a reward-bonus incentive program for new, productive ideas.
- Give people some free time for individual or group creative problem solving.
- Devise a new form of staff meetings that will let people free-wheel, brainstorm, or flow easily with new ideas.
- Form new or unusual short-term groupings to allow people to cross-fertilize their thinking.
- Have a laboratory, workshop, or "think tank" with necessary materials for tinkering, thinking, and planning.
- Conduct performance reviews that support and encourage creative efforts, ideas, and actions.
- Implement a policy that reduces fear of making a mistake if one tries something different.
- Keep people openly informed about the problems in the organization that need solving.
- Have a reward and recognition system for the creative person.
- Ask an outside person to observe current organization functioning to assess creative output and suggest ways of improving innovation.

- Have a team-development session with the special focus of improving the creative atmosphere and output of the department or unit.
- Rotate people into different positions or parts of the organization, so there is a new mixture of people working on old problems.
- Organize a job enrichment session where people devise ways of enriching their own jobs.

The group or groups responsible for planning action should consider these and any other alternatives before putting them together into a plan of action.

Creative Exercises in Planning

One possible exercise at a group meeting would be to introduce some new, creative ways of planning that have not been tried before.

- Have a brainstorming session. See how many different suggestions can be produced by stimulating creativity in the work unit.
- Have the group spend time looking at possible new products, new services, or new ways of doing work.
- Give people time to discuss a new idea or approach they may have thought of.
- It may be possible to engage in some group creativity training. With resource help, look at the elements of individual and group creativity and spend a day in practicing such creativity-developing activities as brainstorming, developing analogies, seeing parallels and symbols, and exercises on group problem solving.

The team that is bogged down in complacency, or that fails to use its creative talent effectively, is in danger of falling behind its more creative competition at an increasing rate. Team development for such groups should be centered on breaking these units out of familiar ruts and creating conditions for expanded innovation. This means building in organizational supports for stimulating more creative effort, and also providing some experience in new ways to solve problems and perhaps some training in the creative process.

Increasingly, those who analyze organizations are finding that the underlying cause of much low-level output and dissatisfaction among workers is not the authoritarian boss, but the passive boss and the complacent work group. As we continue to graduate more students with specialized training at the baccalaureate level and advanced degrees, these bright, well-trained young people are going to demand work settings that offer challenge, stimulation, and a chance to use their creativity on the job.

Recently, much analysis has been done to study innovation in organizations. Clifford and Cavanagh[3] have looked closely at midsize companies and found that successful ones were characterized by an emphasis on experimentation and innovation. Much of this spirit must come from the organization head or chief executive officer. In the team framework, this means that the top executive team must set the pattern of innovation and encourage this as an organization norm down through the teams that are linked below.

The high-performing organizations are able to emphasize the following norms that must become standards of behavior in every team.

- Everyone has a sense of mission and shares common values.
- They pay attention to business fundamentals.
- They treat bureaucracy as the enemy.
- They encourage experimentation.
- They stay close to their customers and work for them.
- They put motivation and development at the top of their priorities.

These conditions must be built into every team, starting from the top and continuing down to the working teams on the shop floor.

It has been shown that sometimes in organizations there is a dilemma about creativity that starts at the top and trickles down. The dilemma is that sometimes the person who has founded the organization and nurtured its growth wants everyone else to conform to his pattern, and only the head of the organi-

---

[3]D. Clifford and R. Cavanagh, *The Winning Performance: How America's High-Growth, Mid-Size Companies Succeed* (New York: Bantam Books, 1985).

zation is allowed to be innovative. Such a pattern seems to be destined to develop an organization that is conforming and non-creative, and just the opposite of the spirit that made the organization originally successful.

It is very difficult for one team in a high-conforming organization to try to become more innovative if the organization does not accept and reward their new, more imaginative ways of functioning. Team creativity seems to be best achieved if it is part of a pattern in the whole organization.

11

Reducing Interteam Conflict

Thus far this volume has concerned itself with designs and methods for increasing the team effectiveness *within* a work unit. It is often the case that a major organizational problem is the lack of teamwork between units, not inside a unit. In fact, units of organizations that become too cohesive, too self-involved and concerned, may be ineffective in their working relationships with other units.

Lawrence and Lorsch in their differentiation-integration model have clearly demonstrated that units of organizations are and should be different. When units have differing tasks, goals, personnel, time constraints, and structures, the functioning of these units is bound to be different. The issue is not how to make all units the same, but how to develop an integrating process that allows these contrasting units to work together. One strategy for bringing greater integration between work units is an interteam development program.[1]

---

[1]The basic theory and method for intergroup processes is found in R. Blake, H. Shepard, and J. Mouton, *Managing Intergroup Conflict in Industry* (Houston: Gulf, 1954). For other discussions on intergroup building strategies see: J. K. Fordyce and R. Weil, *Managing with People* (Reading, Mass.: Addison-Wesley, 1971), pp. 123–130; R. Beckhard, *Organization Development: Strategies and Models* (Reading, Mass.: Addison-Wesley, 1969); E. H. Schein, *Organizational Psychology* (Englewood Cliffs, N.J.: Prentice-Hall, 1965), chap. 5.

Diagnosing the Problem

An interteam development program may be considered as a possible action when two or more teams, which must collaborate for each to achieve its own unit's objectives, experience one or more of the following conditions:

- Unit members avoid or withdraw from interactions with people from the other unit when they should be spending more working time together.
- The mutual product or end result desired by both units is delayed, diminished, blocked, or altered to the dissatisfaction of one or both parties.
- Needed services between units are not asked for.
- Services between units are not performed to the satisfaction of those in the units.
- Feelings of resentment or antagonism occur as a result of unit interactions.
- People feel frustrated, rejected, or misunderstood by those in the other unit with whom they must work.
- More time is spent in either avoiding or circumventing interaction with the other unit, or internally complaining about the other unit, than in working through mutual problems.

Designing the Solution

If at least one of the managers in the dysfunctional unit interaction diagnoses the situation accurately and is willing to contact the other unit manager, an interunit team-development program may be proposed. It is necessary to get agreement of *both* units to move the program ahead. It has been observed that the managers of the two groups agree to an interteam building process but do not get the commitment of their unit members. This results in the program taking place in the middle of a great deal of resistance.

The goal of the program is to develop a problem-solving

process that will reduce the existing dysfunctional interaction and allow future problems to be solved more effectively before a breakdown in unit interaction occurs. Following are possible design strategies for planning and conducting the proposed program.

In preparation, members of both units should have the purpose and format of the program explained to them. This could be done by the manager involved or in conjunction with an outside facilitator. Agreements to participate should be achieved in both units.

Plans should be made for a block of time to get the appropriate people from both units to work on the interface problems. If the two units are small, it may be possible to involve all unit personnel. If units are larger, it may be necessary to have representatives work through the problem areas.

Design A

1. Appropriate members from units X and Y meet to work out a more functional method of operating. Members are introduced and the plan, purpose, and schedule of the program are reviewed.

2. Establish ground rules. The essential ground rule is that people should agree to adopt a problem-solving stance. The issue is to work out a solution, not to accuse or fix blame. Participants should agree to look at the behavior of their own group members and identify times when their own members are trying to accuse, fix blame, or defend a position rather than solve the problem.

3. Unit members *in their own groups* begin work on the following task. On sheets of newsprint answer the following.

   a. What actions does the other unit engage in that create problems for us? List them.
   b. What actions do we engage in that we think may create problems for them? List them.
   c. What recommendations would we make to improve the situation?

4. Each unit brings its sheets of paper and gives them to the other unit to review.

5. Time is allotted for each unit to review the work of the other unit and to ask questions for clarification. Agreements and disparities in the two lists are noted.

6. Members of the two units are now put into *mixed teams* composed of an equal number of members from both units. The first task is for each team to review the lists and come up with an agreed-on list of the major problems or obstacles that keep the two units from functioning together effectively.

Each mixed team presents its list of problems to the total group and the results are tabulated. The major agreed-on problems are then identified and listed.

7. Members return to the mixed teams. Each mixed team is given one of the problems identified to work out a recommended solution. This should include what the problem is, what actions should be taken, who should be responsible for what actions, what the time schedule is, and how to keep the problem from occurring again.

8. Mixed teams bring their solutions back to the total group for review and agreement, particularly from those who must implement the actions.

Design B

This design is similar to A. However, instead of the two teams doing their work alone and then presenting the sheets to the other, each unit discusses its issues *in front of* the other group. This is a "fishbowl" design.

1. Group X sits together in a circle. Group Y sits outside and observes and listens. Group X members discuss the three questions listed in part 3 of design A. A recorder writes down the points of discussion.

2. Group Y now moves into the center circle. Group X observes and listens.

3. Following the fishbowl, mixed teams are formed and they perform the same tasks as in design A.

Design C

A variation on designs A and B is to have the units discuss different questions. The designs are the same; only the questions are different.

1. How do we see the other unit? What is our image of them?
2. How do we think the other unit sees us? What is their image of us?
3. Why do we see them the way we do?
4. Why do we think they see us as we think they do?
5. What would have to change so we would have a more positive image and interaction with each other?

Design D

1. An outside facilitator interviews members of both units privately prior to the team-development session. He or she tries to identify the problems between the units, the source of the problems, and people's recommended solutions.

2. At the interteam meeting, the facilitator summarizes the results of these interviews. The summaries are printed or posted for all to see.

3. Mixed teams from both units review the summary findings and list the major areas they feel need to be resolved. Major areas are agreed on by the total group.

4. Mixed teams engage in coming up with recommended solutions to the problem assigned to them.

Design E

This design involves selecting a mixed task force composed of members from both units. The job of the task force is to review the interface problems and then recommend solutions to the problems for both groups to consider and agree on.

1. Representatives of the task force are selected in the following manner. Team X lists *all* of its group members who the group feels could adequately represent them on the task force. This list is given to Team Y. Team Y then selects the three or four members from team X they feel would best represent their interests. Both units engage in this listing and selecting process. The result is a mixed task force composed of members agreeable to both units.

2. The task force may work in many ways. They may wish to interview people from the other units. They may wish to invite a facilitator to work with them. Whatever their working style,

they are asked to come up with: the major conditions blocking interteam effectiveness; what actions should be taken; who should be responsible for what actions; time frame; how we can prevent these problems from occurring again or what method we will use for solving other problems that may arise.

Design F

A forcefield model could be used by any combination of the two teams. They agree that the current level of functioning is not adequate. Then they agree they need to improve to a higher level of cooperation. The two groups list and agree on the major restraining and driving forces. In subgroups they look at the major forces and develop actions for dealing with these forces agreeable to all.

Discussion

Since a variety of interteam building models are available, what determines which model would be most appropriate? One factor to consider is the confidence and competence of the unit managers to conduct such a program alone, without the help of an outside facilitator. If they choose to conduct the session alone, it would be wise to select an alternative that is simple, easy to communicate to others, with minimal chance for slippage in the implementation. Design E, the selection of an interteam task force, is the most traditional way to work on the interteam problems and is probably the easiest alternative to implement without help. It is also the design that has the least involvement of all the members of the two groups and may have the least impact, at least initially.

Design A probably is the most straightforward problem-solving format with the least possibility of surfacing conflicts and issues that could erupt into an unproductive rehash of old grievances. The fishbowl design may create reactions to individuals as they are observed that may be difficult to handle without a trained facilitator, and approaching the issue via an examination of mutual images (design C) may also give rise to feelings and reactions that may be disruptive to one not used to handling such concerns.

Conclusions

Intergroup problems open up the issue about the unit as to which one has commitment and what is the ultimate "team." In modern organizations, it is not enough to build intense loyalty into the work unit or department, particularly at the expense of the larger organization. Unless people in different departments that must collaborate can see the larger picture and understand that the team is more than the small group, intergroup conflicts can and do emerge. Team-building sessions *between* units can be conducted before problems occur to cement relationships and establish working guidelines. Certainly it is important to get work units together and iron out difficulties when intergroup problems occur. Single-unit loyalty can be detrimental to achieving the organization's goals.

Part IV

Special Issues and Opportunities Facing Teams Today

12

Overcoming Unhealthy Agreement

At times teams bog down, not out of conflict that is open, but because people pretend to agree when they really do not, as illustrated by the following incident:

The Abilene Paradox[1,2]

July Sunday afternoons in Coleman, Texas (population 5607) are not exactly winter holidays. This one was particularly hot — 104 degrees as measured by the Walgreen's Rexall Ex-Lax Temperature Gauge located under the tin awning that covered a rather substantial "screened-in" back porch. In addition, the wind was blowing fine-grained West Texas topsoil through the house. The windows were closed, but dust filtered through what were apparently cavernous but invisible openings in the walls.

---

[1]Much of the material in the section entitled "The Abilene Paradox" was contained in the article by J. Harvey, "Managing Agreement in Organizations: The Abilene Paradox." Reprinted by permission of the publisher from *Organizational Dynamics*, Summer 1974. © 1974 by AMACOM, a division of the American Management Association.
[2]With Jerry Harvey.

"How could dust blow through closed windows and solid walls?" one might ask. Such a questions betrays more of the provincialism of the reader than the writer. Anyone who has ever lived in West Texas wouldn't bother to ask. Just let it be said that wind can do a lot of things with topsoil when more than thirty days have passed without rain.

But the afternoon was still tolerable — even potentially enjoyable. A water-cooled fan provided adequate relief from the heat as long as one didn't stray too far from it, and we didn't. In addition, there was cold lemonade for sipping. One might have preferred stronger stuff, but Coleman was "dry" in more ways than one; and so were my in-laws, at least until someone got sick. Then a teaspoon or two for medicinal purposes might be legitimately considered. But this particular Sunday no one was ill; and anyway, lemonade seemed to offer the necessary cooling properties we sought.

And finally, there was entertainment. Dominoes. Perfect for the conditions. The game required little more physical exertion than an occasional mumbled comment, "shuffle 'em" and an unhurried movement of the arm to place the spots in the appropriate perspective on the table. It also required somebody to mark the score; but that responsibility was shifted at the conclusion of each hand so the task, though onerous, was in no way physically debilitating. In short, dominoes was diversion, but pleasant diversion.

So, all in all it was an agreeable — even exciting — Sunday afternoon in Coleman; if, to quote a contemporary radio commercial, "You are easily excited." That is, it was until my father-in-law suddenly looked up from the table and said with apparent enthusiasm, "Let's get in the car and go to Abilene and have dinner at the cafeteria."

To put it mildly, his suggestion caught me unprepared. You might even say it woke me up. I began to turn it over in my mind. "Go to Abilene? Fifty-three miles? In this dust storm? We'll have to drive with the lights on even though it's the middle of the afternoon. And the heat. It's bad enough here in front of the fan, but in an unairconditioned

1958 Buick it will be brutal. And eat at the cafeteria? Some cafeterias may be okay, but the one in Abilene conjures up dark memories of the enlisted men's field mess."

But before I could clarify and organize my thoughts even to articulate them, Beth, my wife, chimed in with, "Sounds like a great idea. I would like to go. How about you, Jerry?" Well, since my own preferences were obviously out of step with the rest, I decided not to impede the party's progress and replied with, "Sounds good to me," and added, "I just hope your mother wants to go."

"Of course I want to go," my mother-in-law replied, "I haven't been to Abilene in a long time. What makes you think I wouldn't want to go?"

So into the car and to Abilene we went. My predictions were fulfilled. The heat was brutal. We were coated with a fine layer of West Texas dust, which was cemented with perspiration by the time we arrived; and the food at the cafeteria provided first-rate testimonial material for Alka-Seltzer commercials.

Some four hours and 106 miles later we returned to Coleman, Texas, but tired and exhausted. We sat in front of the fan for a long time in silence. Then, both to be sociable and also to break a rather oppressive silence, I said, "It was a great trip, wasn't it?"

No one spoke.

Finally my mother-in-law said, with some slight note of irritation, "Well, to tell the truth, I really didn't enjoy it much and would have rather stayed here. I just went along because the three of you were so enthusiastic about going. I wouldn't have gone if you all hadn't pressured me into it."

I couldn't believe it. "What do you mean 'you all?'" I said, "Don't put me in the 'you all' group. I was delighted to be doing what we were doing. I didn't want to go. I only went to satisfy the rest of you characters. You are the culprits."

Beth looked shocked. "Don't call me a culprit. You and Daddy and Mama were the ones who wanted to go. I just went along to be sociable and to keep you happy. I would have had to be crazy to want to go out in heat like that. You don't think I'm crazy, do you?"

Before I had the opportunity to fall into that obvious trap, her father entered the conversation again with some abruptness. He spoke only one word, but he did it in the quite simple, straightforward vernacular that only a lifelong Texan and particularly a Colemanite can approximate. That word was "H-E-L-L-L."

Since he seldom resorted to profanity, he immediately caught our attention. Then he proceeded to expand on what was already an absolutely clear thought with, "Listen, I never wanted to go to Abilene. I was sort of making conversation. I just thought you might have been bored, and I felt I ought to say something. I didn't want you and Jerry to have a bad time when you visit. You visit so seldom I wanted to be sure you enjoy it. And I knew Mama would be upset if you all didn't have a good time. Personally, I would have preferred to play another game of dominoes and eaten the leftovers in the icebox."

After the initial outburst of recrimination we all sat back in silence. Here we were, four reasonable sensible people who, on our own volitions, had just taken a 106-mile trip across a Godforsaken desert in furnacelike temperatures through a cloudlike dust storm to eat unpalatable food at a hole-in-the-wall cafeteria in Abilene, Texas, when none of us really wanted to go. In fact, to be more accurate, we'd done just the opposite of what we wanted to do. The whole situation seemed paradoxical. It simply didn't make sense.

At least it didn't make sense at that time. But since that fateful summer day in Coleman, I have observed, consulted with, and been a part of more than one organization that has been caught in the same situation. As a result, it has either taken a temporary side-trip, and occasionally, a terminal journey to Abilene when Dallas or Muleshoe or Houston or Tokyo was where it really wanted to go. And for most of those organizations, the destructive consequences of such trips, measured both in terms of human misery and economic loss, have been much greater than for the Abilene group.

This story is concerned with a paradox, "The Abilene Paradox." Stated simply, it is as follows: Organizations frequently take actions in contradiction of what they really want to do and therefore defeat the very purposes they are trying to achieve. It also deals with a major corollary of the paradox, which is that *the inability to manage agreement is a major source of dysfunction* in organizations from the team level up to the total organization.

When a team gets lost in such a cloud of unrecognized agreement, it frequently manifests behavior that leads one to believe, mistakenly, that the unit is caught in a dilemma of conflict. For that reason, it takes a different type of team-development problem-solving process involving agreement management to develop new, more functional organizational behaviors.

Symptoms of the Problem

Since the surface symptoms (that is, conflict) of both agreement and disagreement are essentially similar, the first requirement is to be aware of the symptoms of an agreement-management dilemma. Then, on the basis of correctly identifying the symptoms, one can take functional corrective action.

Harvey[3] has identified two sets of symptoms. The first set can most easily be identified by someone outside the system under scrutiny. In effect, being free of the blinding forces of action anxiety, negative fantasies, existential risk, and the psychological reversal of risk and certainty, all of which contribute to the paradox's pernicious influence, the outsider can frequently observe symptoms hidden by the dust that is all too familiar to residents of Abilene.

The second set, more subjective in character, can be more easily recognized by persons living within the system.

---

[3]J. Harvey, "Managing Agreement in Organizations: The Abilene Paradox," *Organizational Dynamics* (Summer 1974):63–80.

Symptoms More Easily Observable to Outsiders

Outsiders, whether detached laymen or professional consultants, can be relatively sure that the team is on a trip to Abilene if they observe the following symptoms:

1. Team members feel pain, frustration, feelings of impotence or sterility when trying to cope with the problem. In gross terms, there is a lot of apparent conflict.
2. Members agree privately, as individuals, as to the nature of the problem facing the organization.
3. Members also agree, privately, as individuals, as to the steps required to cope with the problem.
4. There is a great deal of blaming others for the conditions they are in.
5. People break into subgroups of trusted friends to share rumors, complaints, fantasies, or strategies relating to the problem or its solution.
6. In collective situations (group meetings, public memoranda) members fail to communicate their desires and beliefs to others accurately. In fact, they frequently communicate just the opposite of what they mean.
7. On the basis of such invalid and inaccurate information, members make collective decisions that lead them to take actions contrary to what they personally and collectively want to do.
8. As a result of such counterproductive actions, members experience even greater anger, frustration, irritation, and dissatisfaction with the organization.
9. Members behave differently outside the organization. In other situations (families, churches, other work units), they are happier, get along better with others, and perform more effectively.

Symptoms More Easily Observable to Insiders

Likewise, some symptoms, stemming primarily from one's subjective experiences within the team, are more easily identified by persons who are caught up in the problem of mismanaged agreement. For example, if you experience the following feelings within your work unit, you may be pretty sure you are lost in a dust storm of agreement and are on a trip to Abilene.

1. You feel pained, frustrated, impotent, sterile, and basically unable to cope when trying to solve a particular organizational problem.
2. You frequently meet with trusted associates over coffee, clandestine lunches, or in the privacy of your home or office to discuss the problem, to commiserate and to plan fantasized solutions that you would attempt "if the conditions were only right." (Fortunately or unfortunately, depending on your point of view, they seldom are.)
3. You blame others, the boss, other divisions, or those "unperceptive people in Unit X" for the dilemma. The boss, in particular, frequently gets an unequal share of the blame and is described with such statements as "He's out of touch," "She's lost control of the unit," or "He sure as heck isn't as good as Mrs. Watson was in dealing with problems like this."
4. In collective meetings where the problem is discussed you are frequently cautious, less than candid, and vague when discussing your ideas regarding the problem and its solution. Stated differently, you frequently try to determine what others' positions on the issues are without clearly revealing your own.
5. You repeatedly find that the problem-solving actions you take, both individually and collectively, not only fail to solve the problem, but also tend to make it worse.
6. You frequently hold fantasized conversations with yourself on what you might have done — or should have done. "When he said . . . , I wish I would have said. . . . "
7. Finally, you frequently look for ways to escape by taking sick leave, vacation, traveling, or scheduling other "more important meetings" on days when the problem is going to be discussed.

Only when someone in the work unit becomes aware of either or both sets of symptoms does it become possible to design a problem-solving process designed to break out of what is ultimately a self-defeating organizational process.

Team Development Around the Crises of Agreement

Since an essential cause of the hidden-agreement syndrome is that team members are afraid to "own up"[4] to their basic concerns, coping with hidden agreement in work groups is especially difficult. That difficulty, in turn, stems from three essential dilemmas: (1) it involves risk and takes skill for an individual to "own up" to his/her true feelings and beliefs about an issue when other members of the team have publicly taken different and/or contrary positions; (2) it involves risk and takes skill for others to "own up" to their similar private feelings and beliefs, because of their negative fantasies of the terrible consequences that might occur if they reveal them in an unequivocal manner; (3) it is very difficult to learn the individual and collective skills required, even if one is willing to accept the risks.[5]

In summary, the possibility that a work unit could exhibit public equanimity, private turmoil, and perform ineffectively is one compelling reason for work groups to hold periodic team review and development sessions when symptoms of the Abilene Paradox are present. Another reason is that the organization might be able to do something constructive about the problem, even though the skills required for success in such a session may not be easy or comfortable to learn.

The manner in which such review and development sessions might be conducted is next discussed.

---

[4]The term *own up* has a very precise meaning. Essentially *owning up* is (1) a first-person statement beginning with the word *I* ("I think," "I believe," "I want") in which the individual (2) clearly communicates his/her own ideas and feelings about an issue (3) in a descriptive way, (4) without attributing an idea, a feeling, a belief, or a motivation to another.

[5]See C. Argyris, *Intervention Theory and Method: A Behavioral Science Approach* (Reading, Mass.: Addison-Wesley, 1970); and C. Argyris and D. Schon, *Theory in Practice* (San Francisco: Jossey-Bass, 1974).

Format Possibilities for Agreement-Management Team-Development Sessions

There are a number of possible formats for taking action to solve problems. Generally they involve gathering data, sharing theory, and setting norms. Data gathering may be conducted by either insiders or outside consultants. Each approach is described in the following sections.

Data Collection by an Outside Consultant

To bring hidden agreements to light, it may be useful to have an outside consultant interview people in the organization unit. (By an "outside" consultant, we mean someone who is not a part of the blinding, collusive anxiety system that facilitates the hidden-agreement syndrome and who knows the theory and practice of agreement management; in other words, he or she may be a competent professional, friend, or colleague.) Based on the theory of agreement management, such a consultant might ask the following questions: (1) What problem does this organizational unit have that you have a hard time accepting, facing, or discussing? (The question assumes the respondent knows the nature of the problem and can state it.) (2) What decisions or actions have recently been taken regarding the problem that you have not really agreed with? (The question helps determine whether there are consistent discrepancies between private beliefs and public actions, a key symptom of an agreement-management dilemma.) (3) What actions or decisions do you feel would produce the best results for the organization over the long term? (The question assumes the respondent knows an effective solution to the problem.) (4) What will happen if you don't discuss your concerns, feelings, beliefs, and suggestions with all members of the unit who are involved with the problem? What will happen if you do? (The questions assume fantasized consequences either will help or hinder the individual's making a decision to discuss the issue with others in such a way that the problem might be solved.)

Having gathered the data via interviews, the outside consultant would present a summary of their responses simultaneously to them in a group problem-solving session, designed and "contracted" for, essentially, in the manner described by Beck-hard.[6]

Data Collection by Members of the Organization

It is also possible that people from within the organization who are a part of the problem could share data and, by exhibiting such behavior, could encourage others to do the same. In this case, an outside interviewer would not be needed. Again, such data are most effectively shared in a group meeting involving all people key to the problem. In such a meeting, the person who called the meeting explains his or her desire to "own up" and expresses a desire to know others' beliefs and feelings regarding the issue. A typical statement at the beginning of such a meeting might be as follows: "I have some data I want to share with you. I'm anxious about doing it because I may find I'm the only one who sees the problem this way and I don't like to feel alone. But here it is. I really don't think we are going to succeed on Project X. It's important for me to know how others feel about it though. I would appreciate your letting me know what you think."

Despite the competence and good intentions of the person making such a statement, it is possible that the fear element could be so strong that other members of the organization would be unwilling to reveal their true beliefs and feelings; but it is also possible that at least one person would "own up" to his or her concerns and the log jam would be broken. Alternatively, in the absence of such "owning" statements, the probability of the problems being solved is reduced.

Sharing the Theory

In addition to data collection and data sharing, an important element of such problem-solving sessions is for all members of the organization to know the theory of agreement management. To accomplish the goal of communicating theory, the story of "The Abilene Paradox," which opens this chapter, could be distributed to all members of the group prior to the problem-solving

---

[6]R. Beckhard, "The Confrontation Meeting," *Harvard Business Review* (March–April 1967):149–155.

meeting. Each person could be asked to read the story and be ready to discuss whether he or she had experienced or observed any situations in the past or present, or possibly foresaw some in the future, where the organization is (or would be) in danger of taking a trip to Abilene — that is, doing something that no one really wants to do, or not doing something organization members really want to do. Then, at the problem-solving meeting, each person could be asked to discuss The Abilene Paradox and his or her observations of its actual relevance to the work group.

Since the reactions of authority figures set the parameters of other responses in any type of confrontation meeting, it is helpful if the head of the organization can begin the process and can own up to personal concerns about any trips to Abilene that he or she has observed, participated in, led, or may foresee leading.

Agreements, Decisions, and Actions

Once the work group has discussed the theory of hidden agreements and has shared data about any potential agreements that they may be incorrectly treating as conflicts, it is important to come to valid public agreement about the nature of the "true" conditions, make action plans based on the reality of such truths, and then take steps to reduce the probability of future trips to Abilene.

For example, as valid data to the questions are shared, the issues might be summarized and listed on newsprint by a recorder. Then, on the basis of the data so collected and recorded, the work group could discover those hidden agreements (or real disagreements) both about the organization's basic problems and the solutions that might solve them. To "formalize" the process and to facilitate specific actions, they might also formulate a summary statement that captures the essence of their agreements. For example, if they were to discover a hidden agreement that everyone, including the boss, agreed that the regular staff meetings were poorly planned and a waste of time, they might produce the following summary of their agreement: Our weekly staff meetings are not planned well and do not have a clear enough purpose to make them worthwhile.

As each area of potential agreement is collectively owned up to, the group could continue the discussion until it reaches a valid agreement in the form of a written summary statement about the nature of the problem.

Once there is agreement about the problems, the next step is to come to a decision in writing about new courses of action that would help to resolve these dilemmas. These may take the form of new policies, programs, or activities. For example, if organization members bring to light the hidden agreement that staff meetings are a waste of time, they might "formalize" the following actions in a problem-solving statement: In the future, no staff meeting will be held unless staff agrees on the agenda and a special committee chosen by the total staff plans the meeting to increase the probability of its success.

Preventing Future Trips to Abilene

Once the immediate problem of specific hidden agreements has been faced, the next step for the group is to establish a process that will reduce the probability that similar problems will occur in the future. Underlying the paradox of collective consent to the trip to Abilene is fear. Fear, in turn, is a reflection of organization climate, and is both affected by and expressed through negative fantasies. For instance, the climate may be expressed by the fear subordinates express about one powerful person and the manner in which people figuratively tremble because of the fantasies they have about the consequences of disagreeing with that person. Or it may be expressed as fear of a nonspecific group, such as "top management." Such fears can both contribute to and reinforce a general dysfunctional organizational climate, maintained by myths, rumors, and incidents grounded in fact and fancy.

In addressing this question, the team may arrive at a number of possible procedures that may prove helpful. Some typical procedures suggested by organization members are these:

1. Appoint an organization ombudsman who, in one capacity, functions as a clearinghouse for all private matters of concern.
2. Periodically invite an external consultant in to interview people about unspoken concerns.

3. Hold regular team-building meetings following the problem-solving format described in earlier chapters.
4. Form an employee panel whose primary function is to talk with others in order to surface potentially controversial concerns and send them in writing to all members of the organization involved in the problem.
5. Make available a form that anyone can fill out anonymously to describe concerns he or she feels personally, but is afraid to share publicly. If more than one person describes the same concern, a meeting is held among the affected parties to discuss the issue or concern.

Although many organizations try such measures, we find that, by themselves, they are effective in the short run but ineffective over the long haul. Their ineffectiveness stems from the fact that, in each of the five procedures, only a minority of the organization — the ombudsman, the internal consultant, and the panel members — have to be both competent and willing to take risks. In fact, one could argue that others in the organization might become more incompetent and irresponsible as a result of having such "crutches" available. (No need in my saying anything — "I'll just let the ombudsman or the employee panel handle it.")

For that reason we prefer an approach where all members learn the extremely difficult skills of owning up, openness, and experimentation, all of which facilitate a climate that fosters individuality (rather than conformity), concern (rather than antagonism), and trust (rather than distrust).

In short, if the question of hidden agreement is to be truly solved, the question to be addressed is this: What skills can team members learn individually and collectively that will allow them to rely at all times on the validity of what other members say? If everyone in the team can learn such skills, then the responsibility for both the defeats and victories in the area of organization decision making can be honestly and productively shared.

13

People Problems in Teams

When a team-development effort is first introduced into an organization, one can anticipate a series of common concerns, areas of resistance, and blocks to progress. People hesitate to start a new program for many reasons. Some fear it will have negative consequences for them. Other ask: Is the time taken worth the effort expended and the results obtained? Is this just another fad of management that will play itself out, only to be replaced by a new contrivance? Rumors may have been circulated about team building having negative effects. Or, people may simply feel awkward and unskilled in the new activity. These are common problems that generally can be handled by holding preliminary meetings to explain in detail the purpose and format of the program and to allow people to express concerns and deal with feelings of resistance.

However, certain special problems or issues may still present a serious roadblock even to starting a team-development program. These can be handled prior to starting the program or built into the design; in this way, the concern can be *appropriately* dealt with during the program.

When the Boss Is the Major Problem

It is not infrequent that the biggest obstacle to a working unit's functioning as a team is the boss or manager. If the boss is unaware of this, the situation becomes especially difficult, since unit members are often unwilling to confront the boss with the disruptive consequences of his or her own managerial behavior. If this issue is avoided during the team-building session, all other actions will probably be seen as mere window dressing, for the main issue has been carefully sidestepped. How do you get at the problem manager? He or she may exhibit a streak of authoritarianism, or may be seen as untrustworthy, manipulative, incompetent, punitive, vindictive, withdrawn or isolated, timid and afraid to take action, outdated in management approach, too busy, or any one of a number of other things. Since the boss is the problem's center, people may feel that any team-building effort is useless unless the boss makes some changes — yet they remain reluctant to raise the issue with the boss for fear of negative consequences. It may also be that they are fond of their boss, recognize these weak spots, and are afraid to point them out for fear it will "hurt" the boss in some way or disrupt their good boss-subordinate relationship.

Certain actions are available to focus on the problem boss and minimize the risk to the rest of the group. Most of these actions involve helping the manager gain some insight into his or her impact on others — the possible negative effects he or she is having — *prior* to beginning the team-building program. If the manager can be helped to initiate this role analysis in the unit, it is considerably easier for subordinates or co-workers to respond, without fear of unpleasant consequences.

Laboratory Training

Through the years, one of the best methods for preparing a manager to begin a program of planned change in his or her own organization has been for the manager to attend a laboratory program centered on experience-based learning. Argyris[1] described

[1]C. Argyris, "T-Groups for Organizational Effectiveness," *Harvard Business Review 42*, no. 2 (March–April 1964): 60–74.

the functions of a T-group for executives and the literature abounds in detailed descriptions of laboratory education.[2] A number of reputable organizations conduct laboratory programs for managers — National Training Laboratories, Behavior Science Resources, University of California at Los Angeles, University Associates, Scientific Methods, the American Management Association, plus many more universities and training and consulting organizations.

A primary objective in any laboratory program is to help the participating managers clearly look at their own behavior, see some of their blindspots, and begin to understand the utility of interpersonal feedback and group problem solving, and to start them thinking about how to improve their actions back home. A good laboratory program is an excellent way to prepare the "problem" manager to start a team-development program. How do you persuade a manager to go to the training program? There's the rub. If a manager doesn't feel he or she needs the program or is too threatened to participate, it is difficult to force the issue.

Some companies regularly have their managers attend a laboratory program as a basic experience for everyone, assuming that the problem manager will be stimulated enough to follow up with a "back-home" program provided the company is encouraging ongoing team development. Laboratory training without some systematic follow-up activity in the back-home organization tends to have only sporadic long-run benefits to the organization.

A variety of other methods have been used to suggest to a problem manager that laboratory or some other training would be a helpful prelude to some intensive development work with the total unit. Sometimes the role of the personnel manager is to pick up data from people in a manger's unit about the manager's need for additional training. The personnel manager may then make recommendations to the manager. In-company surveys may point out the need for some managers to have additional exposure to training methods designed to help them see themselves more

---

[2]See L. P. Bradford, J. R. Gibb, K. O. Benne, *T-Group Theory and Laboratory Method* (New York: Wiley, 1964); and E. Schein and W. Bennis, *Personal and Organizational Change Through Group Methods* (New York: Wiley, 1965).

clearly. The function of an outside consultant may be to recommend needed training. Third-party facilitators (another manager, a higher level manager, a friend) may have data about a manager's performance which will prompt them to suggest further training. And it has even been known for a group of subordinates to suggest to their boss that he or she might benefit from a week in a T-group.

Management Profiling

A newer method for preparing a manager for starting a team-building effort is management profiling. This procedure involves gathering data via instruments about the manager from his or her subordinates, peers, and superior. The data is then summarized and presented to the manager for analysis. These data, if properly and honestly completed, will help the manager see — in private — the areas of concern, and can prepare the manager psychologically for self-analysis.

Organizations offering profiling procedures, with instruments and methods for helping a manager get more insight, include Behavior Science Resources (BSR), Telometrics, Scientific Methods, and 3-D, among others. Usually in this process, a person from outside the manager's unit (a personnel person from the company or an outside consultant) is in charge of administering the instruments, preparing the summary, feeding the data back to the manager, and helping the manager plan the next step, which is often some form of feedback of results to the total work group, which then begins a team-building program.

Again, the problem is to induce the manager to engage in a profiling procedure. Methods similar to those described above for stimulating attendance at a laboratory are commonly used.

Interviewing or Surveys

Many organizations have available one or two common data-gathering procedures designed to uncover problems in the organization. One is to have an outsider come in and interview people about conditions in the work unit, a procedure that could easily reveal some problem with the boss. The advantage of this process is that it allows the boss to review the data and prepare to begin a program, for without the information he or she may not recognize a need or be prepared to move ahead. An organization survey instead of personal interviews is another method with similar results.

The Use of an Honest Observer

Any manager might well assume that certain parts of his or her management style create problems for others. To make sure that these areas are confronted in a team-building session, the manager may wish to invite in a subordinate, co-worker, or a forthright observer and ask, in confidence, what that person sees as the areas that the manager needs to examine in helping build a better working relationship with the work group.

Dealing with the Problem-Manager Issue

Assuming that the manager has some difficulties with the staff and that they are reluctant to raise the issue out of fear, mistrust, or overconcern, and assuming that the manager has taken one of the above steps and now wants to deal directly with the issue of personal effectiveness, how can this be handled? Probably the least threatening process is for the manager to ask — and the subordinates to give.

If a manager asks, "What about my style don't you like or what gives you trouble?" subordinates may feel very uncomfortable replying candidly. However, if the manager asks, "Do you have any suggestions about how I might improve our staff meetings (or our decision making, or our planning, etc.)?" suggestions are likely to be forthcoming. To respond about what one likes or dislikes forces some kind of judgment or evaluation, but the giving of suggestions is more likely to be perceived by the asker and giver as a helpful activity with less implicit threat.

Two-Party Conflicts

Sometimes a major disruptive element in a work unit is a problem between two people, two co-workers or the boss and a subordinate. If such is the case, the rest of the team members would like to see the differences resolved but may feel it inappropriate to deal with the issue in front of the whole group. It is often more useful for the team if the two members get together privately sometime during the team-building program and work on their differences. Walton[3] shows how helpful a third-party facilitator can be in dealing with such matters. The persons involved should communicate to the rest of the group something of the nature of their resolution, particularly if the group has identified the interpersonal conflict as a problem.

This issue should not be confused with a problem that may concern that manager and the total group, with one person being the spokesman for the whole. In this case, it may be better for the manager and the spokesman to deal with the issue with the others present, with the ground rule that only the spokesman shall participate in the exchange. A time-out could be called if the spokesman wishes to confer with the others, or if the manager feels it necessary to get more data or authority from his or her boss.

The Problem Member

One of the most common questions asked is, "What do you do when you have one member of the team who continually blocks the rest of the unit? This member may always take a contrary point of view, vote against proposals everyone else supports, take a negative or pessimistic position on everything, and frequently will miss meetings or not follow through on assignments."

The obvious question in response is, "Why do you keep a person like that in your organization?" Usually the answer is that this person has some needed competencies, is a long-time employee, and termination or transfer have a lot of built-in problems. However, if a manager or supervisor is trying to build a team and one person won't buy into the process, some method of eliminating that person should be considered.

The following kinds of action have also been found to be successful in some (not all) cases.

Direct Confrontation Between the Team Leader and Problem Person. This may give the superior an opportunity to

---

[3]R. Walton, *Interpersonal Peacemaking* (Reading, Mass.: Addison-Wesley, 1969).

describe clearly the problem behaviors and the consequences if such behaviors do not change.

Confrontation by the Group. If it is the boss only who deals with the problem person, the conflict may be perceived by that person as just the personal bias of the boss. In a case like this it would be better for the group collectively, in a team meeting, to deal directly with the problem member. The ground rules are: Be descriptive, not evaluative. Describe the problem behavior and identify the negative consequences of the behaviors, and all this without punitive, negative evaluations of the individual personally.

Special Responsibility. It has been found for some difficult people that giving them a more controlling role in the team increases their commitment to the team process. The person might be asked to be the team recorder, the agenda builder, or the one to summarize the discussion of issues. One team even rotated the difficult member into the role of *acting* team leader with the responsibility for a limited time of getting team agreement on the issues at hand.

Limited Participation. One team asked the problem person to attend meetings, listen but not participate in the team activities, and then have a one-to-one session with the team leader. If the leader felt the member had some legitimate issues to raise, they would be presented by the leader to the group at the next meeting, but in all cases the discussion of the team would be final.

External Assignment. At times it may be possible to give the problem person an assignment outside the activities of the rest of the team. The person may make a contribution to the work unit on an individual basis while the bulk of the work that requires collaboration is handled by the rest of the team.

All of the above represent suggestions when the person is a real obstruction to the working of the group. One must always be careful to differentiate the real problem person from a person who sees things differently and whose different views or perspectives need to be listened to and considered with the possibility that this may enrich the product of the team. Teams can get too cohesive and isolate a person because he is different — not because he is a problem.

Minority Group Members

One of the current concerns facing many organizations is the matter of minority-group activities and women's rights. Sometimes a team will handle these matters entirely within its own normal group processes. The issue gets raised and the group makes the necessary adjustments to deal with these sensitive matters. When discrimination of any kind is present that is directed toward a team member, some action increases. If normal procedures do not deal with the issues there may be a need to pull the unit together for a special team-building meeting around the new concern.

The format of such a special meeting should always be focused on the problem and action to solve it. If the matter of racism were raised, it would hardly be productive to spend time in making charges and countercharges as to who is or is not racist. The problem-solving stance should be: "What actions do we need to take to eliminate any feelings that racism occurs in our team?" Then the focus of the group's attention is on planning and action taking — not on name calling or derisive confrontation.

14

When Team Building Should Not Be Used

Should Everyone Use Team Building?

It seems obvious that all work units are not "teams" in the sense that the people involved must work together to achieve results. How do you determine whether or not this new methodology of team development is appropriate for your situation? In a thoughtful article, Lewis[1] identifies certain basic assumptions which, if not met, would suggest that team building would not be appropriate. He says:

> Team development and a decision to pursue it in an organization rest on a number of critical implicit assumptions. It is worthwhile to identify them, since if one or more of these assumptions do not apply to a particular management group or its situation, undertaking a team development effort may be unnecessary, detrimental, or both.

[1] John W. Lewis III, "Management Team Development: Will It Work for You?" Adapted by permission of the publisher, from "Management Team Development: Will It Work For You?", *Personnel*, July/August 1975, pp. 14, 15, 21, 24, 25. © 1975 American Management Association, New York. All rights reserved.

- Current patterns of communication and interaction among members of a group are inadequate for group and organizational needs.
- The concept of being (or desiring to be) an integrated team exists in the minds of the executive and managers in the group.
- Significant face-to-face interaction among members of the group is expected by the executive and/or required by the needs of the organization.
- The executive can and will behave differently as a result of the development effort, and team members can and will respond to his new behavior.
- The organizational tasks assigned to the group require close and frequent coordination laterally among group members in such matters as planning, problem solving, and decision making.
- The benefits in terms of group effectiveness and member satisfaction to be gained from team development outweigh the costs incurred from altering existing role and social network arrangements to which the group has accommodated.

Lewis also points out that team development must be congruent with the manager's own personal style and philosophy of management as to how to use his or her staff. He says that you should use the team approach only if, as the manager, you find:

1. You are comfortable in sharing organizational leadership and decision making with subordinate managers and prefer to work in an egalitarian atmosphere.
2. A high degree of interdependence exists among functions and managers in order to achieve overall organizational goals.
3. The external environment is highly variable and/or changing rapidly.
4. The organization is young and/or undergoing major change, which results in fluid structure, few operating policies and procedures, and emerging role definitions.

The distinction between "line" and "staff" departments is blurred or meaningless.

5. The organization's dominant technologies are relatively new and/or developing rapidly.
6. Broad consultation among your managers as a group on goals, decisions, and problems is necessary on a continuing basis.
7. Members of your management team are (or can become) compatible with each other and are able to create a collaborative rather than competitive working environment.
8. Members of the management team are located close enough to meet frequently and on short notice.
9. You are dependent on the ability and willingness of subordinate managers to resolve critical operating problems directly and in the best interests of the organization as a whole.
10. Formal communication channels are not sufficient for the timely exchange of essential information, views, and decisions among members of the management team.
11. Organizational adaptation requires the frequent use of project management, temporary task forces, and/or ad hoc problem-solving groups to augment conventional organizational structures.

Problems can arise if a manager or an organization-development specialist sees team building as a general activity that all work units should experience. The indiscriminate use of this methodology can have disruptive effects on the unit for whom it is inappropriate; consequently, a generally negative image of team building can emerge, so that those teams that could benefit will shy away from the process. In light of the arguments presented by Lewis and reviewing the whole issue of team development, before any team-building program is started, the following conditions should be assessed.

Is the work unit one where collaborative action is essential for good achievement? If work is done primarily on an individual basis or requires only a limited amount of interaction, personal, one-to-one consultation and planning may be more useful than team development.

Is the manager familiar with and committed to the idea of team improvement? Often the manager in charge does not understand the long-term nature of a team-building program and is not really willing to invest the necessary time, resources, and energy. He or she may be interested in only a one- or two-day program, with the expectation that all problems will then be solved and business can proceed as usual. Should such be the case, the manager needs a clearer orientation to the nature of the program he or she is buying into.

Is there a feeling of "hurt" or a need to see improvement? Team-development programs have limited impact when the motivation to begin such a program stems from the push of the training department, a need to spend training and development funds before they are lost, or the advice of someone who has heard about the process and thinks it might be a "good thing for us."

Are members of the work unit willing to look at their own unit and engage in problem-solving actions? Where there is low interest in the examination of processes or in honestly analyzing how things are in the work unit, team-building activities are a risk. Low interest can stem from fear, apathy, or cynicism, expressed in such remarks as "Nothing ever really happens around here. We start things but never complete them."

Do personnel have enough time for such a program? Sometimes there is need for and interest in team development, but people are (or they feel they are) too busy with deadlines, projects, or other demands to launch a new program. Before the start of a team-building program, the key people must be interested and have the time available to be involved.

Are the manager and others in the work unit willing to look at their own performance and the work of the unit, willing to give and receive feedback, and honestly interested in making change? Where there is a lack of skill or understanding of the processes of team development, people may find that they have begun a program that involves them in actions they didn't bargain for. Team building often requires people to take a hard look at what they are doing. It often means somebody has to make changes. People may receive disturbing feedback. Awareness of these possibilities and some skill in engaging in change processes are highly desirable before team building begins.

Have people already made up their minds what the problems are and what must be done? Team development functions best if there is an openness to data and a willingness to move in the direction the data suggest. If it has already been decided that a certain action must be taken or certain changes made, and if the team-building program is undertaken merely to confirm these moves and make it seem that the people have decided these things for themselves, such actions are usually perceived as manipulative and result in greater resentment, resistance, and cynicism.

Some Cautions in Team Building

Assuming that the above issues have been confronted and honestly appraised positively, and a team-building program begins, certain cautions or guidelines might well be kept in mind.

Team Building Takes Time. You will not see entrenched behaviors and actions turned around early or easily. Action steps must be managed and agreed-on changes must be revised and rewarded regularly to move new behaviors onto a permanent level. One should think of team development as a process that should continue over a period of from one to three years.

People in Power Must Support Changes. Team building as a process will surely not have a long-term impact if people who are in positions of power do not support the solutions to problems suggested by team-development procedures. A manager cannot ask subordinates to spend time and energy wrestling with organization problems and then go about business as usual, ignoring or even blocking the efforts the subordinates were asked to produce. Unfortunately, such has been the case in several team-development efforts. One effective manager took the following stance regarding the actions developed in the team-building sessions. He told his subordinates, "We will set up agreeable terms to review the results of the actions established. Your performance review and the subsequent raises and promotions will be to a large extent contingent on your willingness and ability to implement the actions agreed on." This represents a real commitment on the part of a manager to support the decisions arrived at via the team-building process.

Involvement Enhances Commitment. There is ample evidence to indicate that people will have greater commitment to decisions, goals, and actions they have participated in developing. Managers who impose team-building activities on others and then force or manipulate desired outcomes without allowing honest involvement of group members run the risk of a long-run failure, even though they went through a team-development activity. People should feel that they are honestly involved and listened to, and that their real ideas and concerns are taken into account.

Team Development May Need to Be Done More Than Once. In today's organizations, there is often a great deal of personnel turnover. The composition of a work group can change radically in just a few years. When key personnel in a department are replaced, the new configuration of personalities and perhaps new assignments and expectations may make another team-development process useful if not mandatory. Agreements made with one set of people may not persist with the change of personnel; therefore, the new group may need to go through the whole process again.

Team Building Must Be Rewarded. My research has shown that many organizations want people to function together in a cooperative team. But there is nothing in the organization's formal reward system that indicates there is any payoff for the manager or supervisor who spends the time in team development. There may be nothing in the performance review process that indicates that team building is considered important. If people are going to spend time and energy building a team, they must see that the system recognizes these efforts and is willing to reward them.

15

The Future of Team Building

When the first edition of this book was published in 1977, I predicted that team building would slip into the normal practices of management and it would be taken as a matter of course that all managers would spend time developing the work team. However, ten years later I do not see managers developing team-building skills, although almost every organization supports the notion of teams and teamwork.

Business schools that should be teaching young men and women how to work in teams give lip service to the process but do not know how to teach these skills to prospective organizational managers and workers. The professors may put students into study or project teams and grade the team product but will spend no time at all in helping these students understand how a good team functions and how to manage the group problems that may arise. The end result is that usually a few students take over and get the group paper or project completed while others goof off or slide along and get rewarded for the efforts of others. This leaves many students with a negative feeling about team activities as they leave school and go into the work force.

Yet there seems to be more evidence now than ten years ago that people must cooperate in some way to get work done.

New developments in the business and general organizational world seem to almost demand more effective teamwork. Here are some of the recent activities that seem to require team skills.

Acquisitions and Mergers. In today's business situation one reads almost daily of situations where there is a merger of companies, a buyout of one company by another, and the unfriendly takeover of one company by another. The original transactions in all of these cases are almost always financial in nature; that is, there are financial reasons that make these actions feasible. But in the long term, the success of such activities depends on whether or not the people who are involved can make the new corporate form work. In mergers or acquisitions of any type, the former separate units must come together and form one team with common goals and shared procedures. A continuation of these trends would seem to enhance the need for someone to know how to help these units merge into one.

New Technology. Even though computers have now been around for many years, the uses of the computer and other new technologies are still in the development stages. When an organization is faced with new equipment and new technologies that demand changes, the evidence seems to indicate that change will result sooner and with greater willingness to take risks in a supportive group or team situation than among individuals by themselves.

Work Restructuring. In many industries and organizations, reshaping of the work environment is a necessity. The divestiture of AT&T is a prime example of one company that had a million employees and was forced to reshape its total organization. Other oil companies, in light of the oil glut, were forced to cut back drastically. Again, those units that knew how to involve people in team situations where there was an opportunity to talk and build understanding and support were able to deal better with these new, greatly changed conditions.

Teamwork with Former Adversaries. It has been almost a revelation to watch groups that formerly had an adversarial relationship try to work together in a collaborative stance. One of these situations has been union–management negotiations. Since the first edition of this book we have seen the automobile industry work out entirely new relations with the unions to meet a serious economic crisis. Some other industries were not successful, and businesses closed down because cooperative relations between management and labor could not be achieved. We have seen collaboration between industry and government, with federal and state government supporting companies with financial troubles. It seems likely that with the threat of rising economic power in the developing Third World companies, former adversaries would benefit from learning how to work together as a team.

Cooperation to Solve Social Problems. Today Americans, as well as Western society, face a range of social problems that seem to cry out for collaborative efforts. There are the issues of drugs, emigration and immigration, unemployment, organized crime, population problems, protective tariffs, and import quotas, to name just a few. Such problems will not go away, nor can they be solved by one group alone. It will require people of diverse interests and backgrounds to come together in some form of temporary team to deal with these issues effectively. If team skills are lacking, the problems may not get solved because the people may not know how to work together.

What will the effective organization of the future be like? It is quite likely that these organizations will become more flexible, quicker to shift people to meet the new demands of what has been an increasingly rapidly changing society and world. If such is the case, people will need to learn to form teams quickly — to establish working relationships that are effective and ground rules that are accepted and viable. Only in this way can they get on with the work at hand without getting bogged down in the misery of wheel spinning that characterizes so much of the current work done in organizations.

Organizations of the future may require that a person belong to several units at the same time and have two, three, or even four bosses. People may shift rapidly from one temporary system to another; organizations with managers who know how to build effective teams in a hurry will have a special advantage.

Right now one of the problems of team development in organizations involves dispersal of new ideas. In trying to change the organization's culture, team building has proven to be a rather slow method in terms of spreading the new, more collaborative processes throughout a large organization. It is foolhardy to begin team development at the top of the organization in the hope that managers will make the process trickle down. By the time the lower levels of the organization experience the impact of team building, the top levels have moved to other matters, or the composition of higher teams has changed and the interlocking effect has been lost.

In the organization of the future, certainly new, more innovative methods for introducing team development organizationwide will be available. Already there are experiments in high-spread methods. Some work has been done in training all managers in an organization at once to go immediately into a team-building program — all at the same time. Video and audio tapes have been used to expose all teams to the same set of instructions, examples, and training materials. The methodology for quickly spreading team development through the organization is even now in the growing stages.

Team development does not mean managing by committee, where no one is in charge and all actions must be decided by all. A team is a unified, cohesive group of people who have special functions, but each person needs the resources and support of others to get the job done. Team effort will continue as long as humans must rely on other to achieve results.